HUNGER
NO MORE

DILLON
BURROUGHS

*"I am the bread of life.
Whoever comes to me will never go hungry."*
—Jesus (John 6:35)

1-year devotional journey through the Psalms

NEW HOPE
PUBLISHERS
Gospel-Centered. Missions-Driven.

New Hope® Publishers
P. O. Box 12065
Birmingham, AL 35202-2065
NewHopeDigital.com
New Hope Publishers is a division of WMU®.

Library of Congress Cataloging-in-Publication Data

Burroughs, Dillon.

  Hunger no more : a 1-year devotional journey through
the Psalms / Dillon Burroughs.
     p. cm.
ISBN 978-1-59669-355-5
1. Bible. O.T. Psalms–Devotional literature.
2. Devotional calendars. I. Title.
BS1430.54.B87 2012
242'.2–dc23

                          2012013833

ISBN-10: 1-59669-355-X
ISBN-13: 978-1-59669-355-5

N124108 • 0912 • 2M1

Other New Hope books
by Dillon Burroughs

Not in My Town: Exposing and Ending Human Trafficking and Modern-Day Slavery, with coauthor Charles Powell
(includes DVD)

Thirst No More: A One-Year Devotional Journey

DEDICATION

I dedicate *Hunger No More* to my mother,

whose love supported my first breaths, first steps, and first words. Long before I could hold a pen or type a word, her guiding hand held mine through every moment of childhood. My hands that encourage others through writing today first held her hands. Through her patient prayers and efforts, I now live to influence a new generation through my own family and beyond. If my life helps anyone else during my time on earth, it will be due to her dedication. Without her instruction, I may have never experienced the perfect love of my heavenly Father who offers eternity with Him. Soon this life will pass, yet she and I will enjoy eternity with our Creator in heaven, without distance to separate or time to intervene. Until then, may my life both honor her and our Lord as we seek to show His love to all.

Thank you, Mom!
Your love will never be forgotten.

Contents

9

INTRODUCTION

"The hunger for love is much more difficult to remove than the hunger for bread."
—Mother Teresa

Hunger. The very word evokes images of starving children or street people with cardboard signs. And while physical hunger lingers as one of our world's most pressing needs, there is a deeper hunger that drives every person on the planet. It is not a desire of bread for the stomach, but bread for the soul. According to the words of the Bible, the only One who can truly satisfy spiritual hunger is God.

In my previous devotional *Thirst No More*, I journeyed with readers through the four Gospels to experience the Living Water of Jesus Christ. In this devotional, I've meditated on the Psalms as the portion to satisfy our daily hunger for the Lord Almighty.

Though many believe the Psalms were composed by King David, it is clear by their own acknowledgment that David was only one of the many human authors of this book. Moses, Asaph, King Solomon, and others each contributed inspired lyrics that have been recited and sung by both the Jewish people and Christians for 3,000 years.

In preparation for this book, I found myself reading through the Psalms in English for my 28th time, in addition to much meditation on particular Hebrew words and phrases from the original language of the book. The force of so much time in these inspired texts has enriched my life in an unmatched manner, which I hope will be shared by those who join in reading each day's entry.

The focus of this title is twofold. First, I seek to highlight the words of our Lord presented in the Psalms of the Old Testament. As it reveals, God alone can satisfy our spiritual hunger. Second, I seek to use this privilege to help those less privileged. We live in a world of much need. My friends at WorldCrafts are working to change this crisis. Through providing jobs for artisans in developing nations, lives are being saved every day in the name of Christ. A portion of this book's proceeds is being donated to their efforts. You can read more about their work and how to help in the back of this book or at worldcrafts.org.

Before you begin, let me also share my

desire for this book—*changed lives changing lives.* To my knowledge, my previous devotional book *Thirst No More* was the first devotional that sought to connect its readers in daily online community. *Hunger No More* seeks to continue this pattern. Each day (beginning January 1, 2013), we will experience the privilege to journey together at HungerNoMoreBook.com. I encourage you to share your thoughts each day and to support others who share along the way.

For those like myself who prefer to read on screens or on the go, this book is also available as an ebook and can be read from your computer, ereader, or mobile device. Whether you read it on a screen or in print, you can submit your thoughts to the community from any online device, allowing us to share our daily experiences along the journey from wherever God speaks to you.

Finally, please know I pray for you and all of my readers every day. Your intimacy with Christ is my great pleasure. May you truly experience a life in which you hunger no more because our Lord has become your Daily Bread. May God shine His grace upon you as we share these words together.

"Blessed is the one"
—Psalm 1:1

God's desire for our lives is blessing. However, that blessing is not automatic. There are those who are blessed and those who are not. The difference? The "blessed one" of Psalm 1:1 is the person who is known for a life focused on God.

There are many noble endeavors in this life. Yet the top priority for the one who would be blessed is a diligent allegiance to the Creator of life. As you begin this new year, how would God have you live differently? How would the Lord have you to renew and deepen your pursuit of His ways? If we are to be blessed, we must pursue the Giver of blessings. This year, be the one who is blessed. "Blessed is the one."

Share your experience now at
HungerNoMoreBook.com.

"whose delight is in the law of the Lord."
—Psalm 1:2

Delight is a strong word. We often consider delight as an emotion related to happiness, yet it includes more. To delight in the law of the Lord is to find our source of joy outside of ourselves. Only in the words of God can we truly experience a lasting, enduring delight.

The psalmist found joy in meditating on God's words "day and night." This continual reflection of God's ways in our lives is the starting point and sustaining force of delight in our daily journey. Much trouble may come our way today, yet an ongoing focus on the perfect, inspired words of our Lord will cause us to both endure and enjoy the happenings of our day. Find delight in the law of the Lord.

Share your experience now at
HungerNoMoreBook.com.

JANUARY 3

"For the Lord watches over the way of the righteous."
—Psalm 1:6

We sometimes question whether God is paying attention to our plight. **Where are you God?** is one of the first thoughts that springs into our minds during times of struggle. But the Lord watches over us every moment of every day. He is there—and He cares—about every step and every breath.

Further, the Lord pays particular attention to the lives of those who live for Him. We are told, "The Lord watches over the way of the righteous." He not only sees us, but He guards us along our journey. God keeps His eyes focused on those focused on Him. If your eyes have strayed from your Creator, redirect them anew. There you will find His watchful, loving eyes of love.

Share your experience now at
HungerNoMoreBook.com.

"The One enthroned in heaven laughs."
—Psalm 2:4

Have you ever thought of God as laughing? Often, we consider God as a divine taskmaster, watching our every step for an error He can judge. Yet our Lord is the Creator of joy. In certain moments, "the One enthroned in heaven laughs."

Sometimes, our heavenly Father laughs at the joy His children bring Him, including you. At other times, He laughs at the feeble attempts of His enemies who rebel against Him, as in this psalm. Such efforts can never prevail; God's opponents bring Him no fear. There is no plan that can succeed against the Lord; no strategy that can thwart His ways. Let us join Him in accomplishing His will today rather than our own. Let us bring Him joy, and yes, perhaps even a bit of laughter.

Share your experience now at
HungerNoMoreBook.com.

JANUARY 5

"You are my son; today I have become your father."
—Psalm 2:7

We tend to think of the Psalms as only songs and nothing more. Yet some of its words include predictions of the coming Messiah, including words fulfilled in the life of Jesus. When the psalmist writes, "You are my son; today I have become your father," we are given more than a lyric; we are given a prophecy.

When Jesus came out of the water following baptism, God the Father said, "You are my Son, whom I love; with you I am well pleased" (Mark 1:11). Our worship of God reflects on what He has done, is doing, and will do in the future. God has come to live among us; let us live with Him living through us today.

Share your experience now at
HungerNoMoreBook.com.

"Blessed are all who take refuge in him."
—Psalm 2:12

Refuge was a critical concept in ancient times. During a storm, the refuge of a cave would provide comfort from rain, wind, or snow. In a battle, the refuge of a city would offer safety and security from pursuing enemies, spears, or arrows. Pursuing forces could continue, but they could not prevail. The refuge offered a barrier of protection.

The same is true with God. During life's storms and battles, He is our source of rest and relief. In fact, God's refuge is greater than any physical source of safety. His refuge is not temporary; it is eternal. "Blessed are all those who take refuge in him." God's strength makes us strong; His comfort comforts us. With Him, we no longer run; we rest.

Share your experience now at
HungerNoMoreBook.com.

"But you, LORD, are a shield around me."
—Psalm 3:3

Long ago, a shield was an essential weapon of war. With the spear or sword, an attacker could take the offensive and defeat an enemy. Yet the shield served a different purpose. It provided defense against the weapons of others. Without it, a warrior would stand defenseless against opponents. With it came strength and confidence of victory.

This is what the psalmist indicated when he proclaimed God is "a shield around me." When we are under attack, we need not run from the problems that surround us. God is there, protecting us from harm. With the Lord as our shield, problems are not removed, but we are protected in the midst of them. Today when you face attack, remember: the Lord is a shield around you.

Share your experience now at
HungerNoMoreBook.com.

"Answer me when I call to you."
—Psalm 4:1

We crave answers. Whether it's a test in school or a problem with a relationship, we want to know the outcome and we want to know it now.

This desire for answers is not all bad. A common plea in the Psalms is for God to respond. When the psalmist pens, "Answer me when I call to you," we are given the proper approach. We long for a response, yet turn to God for it. We realize our wisdom is not enough. Only He holds the power to provide the perfect solution.

When we come to God, we need not fear asking for answers. He often uses life's problems to direct us to Him. Let us call to our Lord for the reply we need today.

Share your experience now at
HungerNoMoreBook.com.

JANUARY 9

"In peace I will lie down and sleep."
—Psalm 4:8

Have you ever had trouble going to sleep? Often, the reason has nothing to do with our physical circumstances, but with our spiritual condition. Stress or strife cause our hearts to race, pondering what has taken place in the past or what will take place tomorrow.

Yet the psalmist wrote in confidence, "In peace I will lie down and sleep." How was this possible? It is because of his view of God. When we realize God is bigger than our issues and already holds the solutions, we can rest safely in His arms. We need not neglect the problems of our lives, but we know that our Lord can handle the concerns that overwhelm our spirits. He will be with us through the darkness; let us sleep tonight "in peace."

Share your experience now at
HungerNoMoreBook.com.

JANUARY 10

"In the morning, LORD, you hear my voice."
—Psalm 5:3

Are you a morning person? Many of us are not. We stay under our blankets as long as possible, and then rush as quickly to our destination as a result. Yet the Lord longs to spend time with us even in these often tired moments. "In the morning, LORD, you hear my voice."

Sometimes morning is the best time to talk with God. Before our energy declines or other pursuits distract, He can speak more easily into our calmed souls. Yet we must make an effort to listen. Instead of a morning rush, perhaps God desires a morning reflection with you for the day ahead. Prepare for it, long for it. In the morning, before the day begins, may you hear His voice.

Share your experience now at
HungerNoMoreBook.com.

"But let all who take refuge in you be glad."
—Psalm 5:11

Refuge not only protects; it provides joy. Those who flee for safety in the arms of God find both shelter and gladness: "But let all who take refuge in you be glad."

When we purchase a new item, whether shoes or a house, we know that at some point our purchase will no longer hold the same value. Shoes wear out and even a home will eventually fade in beauty. Yet this is not true with God. When we run to Him, we can take confidence that He will bring joy both now and for eternity. He is a lasting refuge; He provides gladness forever. Do not view the Lord as your temporary solution; see Him as your eternal Savior.

Share your experience now at
HungerNoMoreBook.com.

"Save me because of your unfailing love."
—Psalm 6:4

There is perhaps no word more misused in the human language than love. We love our mother and we also love our favorite food. Yet in each case, we mean something very different. This is perhaps the reason many of the Psalms not only mention love, but also provided details to unpack what is meant by the term.

Psalm 6 asks God to save because of His "unfailing love." The phrase needs little explanation. It is simply love that does not fail. Yet the impact of such love is profound. Even the best human relationships will let us down at times, but God is perfect. His love never fails. We need not fear God will someday mistreat us. He is always there, offering "unfailing love."

Share your experience now at
HungerNoMoreBook.com.

"Save and deliver me from all who pursue me."
—Psalm 7:1

As children, many of us enjoyed playing "tag." There was the person who was "It" and everyone else who would then be chased. The goal, of course, was not to be tagged by the person who was "It." If so, you lost.

When David asked God to rescue him from his enemies, the stakes were much higher. It was no game, but rather life-and-death. David called out to God to keep him from being caught and defeated. Why? He knew God could answer. His Lord was the all-powerful Creator of the universe. David lacked the ability to win, yet knew God could provide victory. Today, do not run in your own strength. Ask for God's help. He can—and will—deliver.

Share your experience now at
HungerNoMoreBook.com.

*"I will sing the praises of the name
of the LORD Most High."*
—Psalm 7:17

Singing is an expression of emotion. Perhaps this is why singing praises to "the name of the LORD Most High" holds such value. In doing so, we are compelled to express feelings that the spoken word simply cannot. Our voices move beyond normal capacity to a heightened degree of passion.

These emotions are not self-centered in the Psalms. Rather, we find the psalmist declaring, "I will sing the praises." The goal was to declare God's worth, not his own. In this we find a powerful truth for our own lives. Our desire must be to express our heart for God and who He is, not our own desires. Only then are we truly praising the One who created us in His image for His glory.

Share your experience now at
HungerNoMoreBook.com.

"When I consider your heavens,
the work of your fingers."
—Psalm 8:3

There is a sense of awe that overtakes us when we look into the starry sky at night. Each light represents a mass larger than our entire planet. Countless stars cover the dark expanse. We feel both small yet majestic at the experience before us.

The psalmist expresses this sense of reverence when he writes, "When I consider your heavens." In the Hebrew perspective, the sky and heavens were communicated using the same word. All that could be seen above was the work of God. Using poetic language, "the work of your fingers" highlights the Lord's personal involvement in this universe-sized work of art, available for all to enjoy. Let us look to the sky today and remember to worship our Creator.

Share your experience now at
HungerNoMoreBook.com.

*"What is mankind that you are mindful of them,
human beings that you care for them?"*
—Psalm 8:4

The same God who created the sun and the moon created you. Does this fascinate you? It certainly overwhelmed the psalmist who asked, "What is mankind that you are mindful of them, human beings that you care for them?" Would the Maker of all things, including every person on the planet, still be able to individually care for each soul?

The answer is a resounding yes. If our Creator can piece together the stars and planets, He can certainly find a way to hear the prayers of His people. The God who created space and time operates beyond these dimensions in a way only He can comprehend. What we can comprehend is that God is there and desires to live in relationship with us today.

Share your experience now at
HungerNoMoreBook.com.

"I will tell of all your wonderful deeds."
—Psalm 9:1

When is the last time you have told someone what God has done in your life? For many of us, it has been too long. Perhaps this was the case of the psalmist who wrote, "I will tell of all your wonderful deeds." It is only natural to share good news with others. Yet with God, His daily blessings are so many that we can easily become numb to their greatness.

The corrective is not to remain silent, but to speak of what the Lord is doing in our lives. When we do, we both praise our heavenly Father and encourage others in the process. In sharing how God is changing our lives, we find the lives of others changed as well.

Share your experience now at
HungerNoMoreBook.com.

"You have upheld my right and my cause."
—Psalm 9:4

When David had won a victory over his enemies, he gave credit where credit was due—to God. In his words, "You have upheld my right and my cause."

Often there is a temptation to take personal credit for the victories in our lives. When we do well at work or succeed in a difficult task, there is a sense in which we think, "Look what I have done!" Yet David's response serves as an example of our proper response. Rather than pointing inward, we are called to point upward to the One who gives us strength to win.

God does care about the victories in our lives; in fact, he is the One who provides them. It is only fitting we honor Him.

Share your experience now at
HungerNoMoreBook.com.

"You, LORD, have never forsaken
those who seek you."
—Psalm 9:10

Many of us wonder if God ever forgets about us. When an answer doesn't come at the time we expect or tragedy strikes, it is easy to question His concern for our lives. But let us not neglect the words of David, "You, LORD, have never forsaken those who seek you."

These words inform us on multiple levels. First, we are never forsaken. There will never be a moment when God is away on vacation. He is always there. Second, we find that the Lord also desires for us to seek Him. He is always there for us; He also longs for us to be always there for Him. Today, let us not doubt His presence; let us desire time in His presence.

Share your experience now at
HungerNoMoreBook.com.

"He does not ignore the cries of the afflicted."
—Psalm 9:12

Life is sometimes painful. There are moments we wish never to repeat nor even remember. Yet these times of struggle also cause us to cry out to the Lord, drawing us closer to Him in the process. "He does not ignore the cries of tthe afflicted."

We would prefer a problem-free life, yet God uses our afflictions to connect us in relationship with Him. When we cry out, He responds. When He responds, we connect at a deep level that helps us through our struggle and beyond. When you face trouble today, do not consider it merely an inconvenience; consider it an opportunity to connect deeply with God. When we do, we'll come through the struggle walking even closer to our heavenly Father.

Share your experience now at
HungerNoMoreBook.com.

"Do not forget the helpless."
—Psalm 10:12

It can seem humorous to remind God not to forget, yet the Psalms do so on multiple occasions. Why? Because from our human perspective, when those who do evil succeed, it causes us to question whether God cares about the hurting. We find ourselves calling out, "Do not forget the helpless."

When we feel helpless, we have no other option than to turn to the Lord. When we turn to the Lord, we connect with Him at a profound level that strengthens our souls. Our weakness reveals God's strength and strengthens us in the process. There is nothing wrong with reminding God to help the helpless. We must simply remember that when helpless, we often find ourselves more mindful of God.

Share your experience now at
HungerNoMoreBook.com.

"The victims commit themselves to you."
—Psalm 10:14

A victim is a person in a position of vulnerability. Victims need protection. When the psalmist writes, "The victims commit themselves to you," one thing is clear: those who need help can find it in the Lord.

In our society, victims are often looked at negatively. Yet God views the needs of victims as opportunities to show His perfect love. In our weakness, He offers His strength. In our pain, He offers His comfort. Those in need can turn to the Lord because the Lord will respond. Today, do not view your weakness as a struggle you must solve on your own. View your weakness as an opportunity to commit yourself to God. In Him, you will find your strength.

Share your experience now at
HungerNoMoreBook.com.

"You are the helper of the fatherless."
—Psalm 10:14

The fatherless formed a special group in Jewish culture. Without a father, there was little help financially, there was little help educationally, and there was a deep sense of loneliness. As a result, many commands of the Torah were directed toward providing for the needs of children without a father.

As He is with others in need of care, God is called "the helper of the fatherless." What they lack, He can provide. This is especially true in responding to the spiritual and emotional issue of loneliness. When we feel alone, God is our help. With Him, we are truly never alone. Our Lord offers perfect fatherly love to all because He is our heavenly Father. He is "the helper of the fatherless."

Share your experience now at
HungerNoMoreBook.com.

"You listen to their cry."
—Psalm 10:17

In the Hebrew worldview, to listen meant more than simply to hear a sound. It included an effort to respond. When the psalmist proclaimed, "You listen to their cry," he had in mind more than a thoughtful ear. He implied a hearing that would answer.

Too often, we think of God as One who listens, yet fails to act. "Why didn't God stop that earthquake?" or "Why did it have to be cancer?" Yet God is ready to intervene at the appropriate time. He is never late and rarely early. He is always exactly on time—His time. We are called to cry out to God with our concerns still today, knowing that He both hears—and responds—as only a perfect Father can.

Share your experience now at
HungerNoMoreBook.com.

*"He observes everyone on earth;
his eyes examine them."*
—Psalm 11:4

God not only sees everything we do, He examines us. We cannot hide from God. Every action, word, and thought are known. The good news is that He can, and will, forgive us when we fail. Further, this knowledge calls us to a deep inspection of our own lives. Do we live as if God was with us at every moment? Do we stop to think He knows our thoughts, even when we do not speak them out loud?

An always-present God presents a difficult dilemma. He sees every misstep, yet His presence also guides each step. Today, let us live mindful that He is with us wherever we go. Let us think, speak, and act in ways that honor Him and those around us.

Share your experience now at
HungerNoMoreBook.com.

"The words of the LORD are flawless."
—Psalm 12:6

David held the highest respect for the words of the Lord. He called them "flawless." What did he mean by this? The parallel in this Psalm 12 compares God's words to gold and silver refined in a crucible. In this process, all impurities were removed so that only the purest of gold or silver remained.

Likewise, God's words are pure and holy. No other writing compares with the inspired expressions revealed from the Creator of the universe. Such awareness must guide us to move beyond a mere respect for Scripture to a consuming reverence for the Bible's words and their impact for our lives today. We must read them, reflect on them, and savor them: "The words of the LORD are flawless."

Share your experience now at
HungerNoMoreBook.com.

"You, LORD, will keep the needy safe."
—Psalm 12:7

The needy of David's time were in constant danger. They often lived without a home and certainly without the security of daily food and water. Every day was steeped in risk. Yet the psalmist declared, "You, LORD, will keep the needy safe."

How could he make this declaration? Because of the words of the Lord. Earlier in this psalm, God had made His will clear. Those in need could turn to God expecting a sure answer. He was there to protect those in need from those who would harm them. The same remains true today. When we stand in need, God not only can keep us safe; he will keep us safe. Let us place our trust in Him, regardless of what life's circumstances bring.

Share your experience now at
HungerNoMoreBook.com.

*"I will sing the Lord's praise,
for he has been good to me."*
—Psalm 13:6

Good news is contagious. We cannot help but pass along the news of a positive medical report or a promotion. When the psalmist experienced an answer from the Lord, he likewise declared, "I will sing the Lord's praise, for he has been good to me."

When we join together with other believers, singing offers us an opportunity to join our voices together in a unique way to offer praise to the Lord. Our voices resound as one voice of thanksgiving for the many blessings He has given to us. Let us sing praise to God today wherever we are, knowing that in doing so we declare the Lord's greatness. His goodness to us compels us to return goodness to Him.

Share your experience now at
HungerNoMoreBook.com.

"The LORD *looks down from heaven on all mankind
to see if there are any who understand,
any who seek God."*
—Psalm 14:2

God not only watches us; He looks for those who would seek Him. As the psalmist acknowledges, there is no one who seeks God on his or her own. We have all fallen short, our sinful nature separating us from our Maker.

Yet this is not the end of the story. Our Creator is also our Savior. He offers salvation to those who believe in His Son by faith. When this psalm was penned, it longed for the day "that salvation for Israel would come out of Zion!" (v. 7). Today, Jesus has come, offering salvation and a relationship with God. Let us thank Him for His salvation andw share it with others, so that God can look down and find many who seek Him.

Share your experience now at
HungerNoMoreBook.com.

JANUARY 30

"Whoever does these things will never be shaken."
—Psalm 15:5

As humans, we long for stability. We crave routine. There is a spiritual sense in which this is true as well. In Psalm 15, David offers us a path that results in, "Whoever does these things will never be shaken."

What are these requirements? Each one listed in the psalm deals with issues of integrity. The one who desires a solid walk with God must live a life beyond reproach. It includes speaking truth, showing love to our neighbors, and honoring the Lord with our lives. There is no secret formula—only a life committed to a close walk with God. Let this be the mark of our lives. Let us not continue a journey along a shaky foundation. Let us walk as those who would never be shaken.

Share your experience now at
HungerNoMoreBook.com.

"You are my Lord;
apart from you I have no good thing."
—Psalm 16:2

With God, we have everything. Without God, we have nothing. This is the simple message of David in Psalm 16: "You are my Lord; apart from you I have no good thing." Even David, king of the entire nation of Israel, realized that without God, He lacked anything of positive value.

If this was true of a national leader, is it not much truer in our lives? We often live as if God does not exist; yet without Him we would not exist. He made us, sustains us, and showers us with a lavish abundance of spiritual blessings. It is only right we call Him our Lord; it is only proper we live as if He is Lord.

Share your experience now at
HungerNoMoreBook.com.

*"My steps have held to your paths;
my feet have not stumbled."*
—Psalm 17:5

The mountainous paths of Israel's countryside wind narrowly along cavernous edges that could cause injury or even death. In biblical times, travelers required focused attention to carefully stay along the solid path of safety rather than tumbling along the sides.

Spiritually, the psalmist declared his steps had remained focused on God's ways too; his feet had not stumbled into dangerous territory. This diligent effort was the desire of God's heart both for the psalmist and for our lives today. His path is solid and secure for our steps. Our goal must be to fix our eyes on His ways, staying clear of sin that could mislead us. God has given us a path; our goal must be to walk with Him on it.

Share your experience now at
HungerNoMoreBook.com.

FEBRUARY 2

"I call on you, my God, for you will answer me."
—Psalm 17:6

Prayer is not a shout, but an echo. When we call to God, we know Someone is there who will hear and respond. When David sang these words to the Lord, he knew his efforts were not in vain: "I call on you, my God, for you will answer me."

David's confidence stands as an example for our prayers. Rather than hoping or wondering if God hears our cries, we can rest assured our petitions are considered and answered according to our Father's perfect will. Even in moments when God may feel distant, we can trust that He is there, prepared with just the right reply to our moment's need. Let us call on the Lord anew today. Let us rely on our Creator's compassion to address our daily needs.

Share your experience now at
HungerNoMoreBook.com.

"The LORD is my rock, my fortress and my deliverer."
—Psalm 18:2

What do a rock, fortress, and deliverer have in common? They are each a source of protection. When David was rescued from Saul, he experienced a very literal redemption from death. The Lord had spared his life from his enemy. As a result, David responded with praise.

He declared the Lord was his rock, a foundation that cannot be broken. David also called his God a **fortress**, a safe location during life's battles. Then he claimed his Father as his **deliverer**, the One who offered victory over his enemies. This same God who spared David's life watches over us today. Let us likewise look to Him as our **rock**, our source of strength in time of need. God is our deliverer.

Share your experience now at
HungerNoMoreBook.com.

FEBRUARY 4

"In my distress I called to the LORD."
—Psalm 18:6

Are you distressed? This feeling of living under intense pressure helped to turn David's attention to the Lord. God continues to use seasons of struggle to direct our eyes toward Him. Perhaps one reason we are experiencing a difficult moment today is to focus our attention on God.

The parallel line in this psalm notes that David's prayer came into God's ears. The imagery is that of David's cry for help entering directly to God so He could respond. Our Father longs to both hear and reply to our needs. Let us offer our concerns to Him at this moment, that we may dwell in His presence and await His response. Let us call to the Lord in our distress; He will meet our need.

Share your experience now at
HungerNoMoreBook.com.

"He reached down from on high and took hold of me."
—Psalm 18:16

Have you ever wished God would reach down and take you away from the mess of your difficult moments? David did. When he called to the Lord for help, David expressed God's answer in this way: "He reached down from on high and took hold of me."

From David's perspective, God's response felt like He had reached down and scooped him up from the intensity of the situation. Rather than overwhelming pressure, David experienced the perfect comfort of a Father holding His son. Such protection saw David through the difficulty of his day and many other difficult days throughout His life. Whatever came his way, David knew God could and would be there to respond. Let us not live in fear, but in faith.

Share your experience now at
HungerNoMoreBook.com.

"My God turns my darkness into light."
—Psalm 18:28

In an age before electricity, fire provided the only human-made light of the night. David mentioned that God kept his lamp from burning out and "my God turns my darkness into light." Here he reveals an attitude that exudes protection and strength. He would not find himself left in the dark. God would give a vision in the darkness and see him through the night.

Many times, we feel as if we walk through dark places. Yet God turns our darkness into light. God operates best in darkness. There His light shines brightest. The difference between light and dark in our lives is not where we stand; it is where God stands with us. With Him, we will always have light for our path.

Share your experience now at
HungerNoMoreBook.com.

"As for God, his way is perfect."
—Psalm 18:30

God is not only good; He is perfect. He has never been wrong and never will be. From beginning to end, He knows all and has planned for everything. Without flaw or fault, He provides exactly the right answer at precisely the right time, every time.

The solution to our human frailty is not to try harder, but to turn Godward. Human efforts can improve our lives, but only God can address our needs apart from mistake. If we wish to truly experience a life that makes an eternal difference, the power within us is not enough. It is the power God offers that matters, a perfect strength He offers to those who turn to Him in faith today: "As for God, his way is perfect."

Share your experience now at
HungerNoMoreBook.com.

"For who is God besides the LORD?"
—Psalm 18:31

We live in a world that speaks of many gods. In fact, there seem to be as many gods or views of these gods as there are people. But David's question remains as relevant today as during his time: "For who is God besides the LORD?"

There is ultimately only one God, one Creator of us all who holds the power to change us and guide our days according to His will. Our first step to experiencing Him in our lives is to acknowledge there is no other God besides Him—and to live accordingly. The One who made us desires to connect with us in relationship. Let us answer the question of "Who is God?" not only with our words, but with our lives.

Share your experience now at
HungerNoMoreBook.com.

"Your right hand sustains me."
—Psalm 18:35

God is more than our Creator; He is also our Sustainer. We focus much attention on the fact that all life came from somewhere; yet we often fail to realize we live each moment of life because of that same source of life—God. When David notes, "your right hand sustains me," we find an acknowledgment of God as the One who both forms and transforms.

As we give praise to God, let us thank Him for giving us life. Let us also thank Him for keeping us alive, savoring each moment as a gift from the Lord. We are created on purpose for a purpose. Today let us life because of Him and live for Him. He is our God whose "right hand sustains me."

Share your experience now at
HungerNoMoreBook.com.

February 10

"The LORD lives! Praise be to my Rock!"
—Psalm 18:46

The only fitting response to God's answers to prayer is praise. We pray, He answers, we praise. This endless cycle of prayer and praise was the ongoing practice of David, a person called a man after God's own heart. As we seek to live as people aligned with His heart, a central focus must be to give praise to God.

Praise is much more than a verbal thank-you note. Praise includes declaring the greatness of who God is. David wrote, "The LORD lives! Praise be to my Rock!" These words reveal our Lord as the Living God. He is a Rock, One offering great strength and security. Let us likewise praise our Father. Let us honor our Lord who lives and stands as our Rock.

Share your experience now at
HungerNoMoreBook.com.

"The heavens declare the glory of God;
the skies proclaim the work of his hands."
—Psalm 19:1

Creation is God's first missionary. The skies reveal a sky-maker. There is no place that has not seen the Lord's glory as unfolded in the design of our natural world. Each of the countless number of stars reflects the beauty of their Designer. Every cloud points toward a majestic Cloud-maker.

When we realize the universal revelation of the skies above, we find a common ground to speak of our Lord to any person in any place. Our God is not hidden. Just look up. He is there. "The heavens declare the glory of God; the skies proclaim the work of his hands." Our God has made Himself known. Let us use His creation to point to our Creator among all who will listen—and look up.

Share your experience now at
HungerNoMoreBook.com.

FEBRUARY 12

"The precepts of the Lord are right,
giving joy to the heart."
—Psalm 19:8

Some things in life are right, but are not enjoyable. We pay taxes because it is required, not because it is fun. We visit the dentist to care for our teeth, not because we usually enjoy the experience.

People sometimes view the Bible in the same way. We are to read it because it's the right thing to do, not because it is fun. Yet the psalmist indicates otherwise. He proclaims, "The precepts of the LORD are right, giving joy to the heart." Scripture is not only right; Scripture brings joy. God's words offer what we need and what we desire. Let us not view the Bible as a requirement to please God; let us view it as a requisite to the pleasures of God.

Share your experience now at
HungerNoMoreBook.com.

"May the LORD answer you when you are in distress;
may the name of the God of Jacob protect you."
—Psalm 20:1

We often wish for protection from trouble. Yet David presents a different perspective—protection during trouble. Why? Perhaps it's because God reveals His best answers when we endure our most difficult situations. When we are in distress, God stands out as our best—and only—answer.

David knew much about living under pressure. He lived as a wanted man, running from his own king in addition to being hunted by neighboring enemy armies. At times it felt like everyone was against him, even those in his own family. Yet the Lord protected him, just as the Lord can do for us today. When in distress, trust in the name of the Lord. He will answer. God will protect us during times of trouble.

Share your experience now at
HungerNoMoreBook.com.

"Some trust in chariots and some in horses,
but we trust in the name of the LORD our God."
—Psalm 20:7

Rather than tanks or drones, ancient armies relied on chariots and horses for military might. With enough of these weapons, an opposing army held little chance of victory. Success was virtually assured.

Yet David understood a greater reality. Though these weapons of war could be helpful, they were not his source of success. In his words, "Some trust in chariots and some in horses, but we trust in the name of the Lord our God." It was God, not human effort, that provided true success. This principle remains true today. Our success is not based on what we do, but on what He can do. Let us not rely on our strength today; let us rely on the Lord to guide us to victory.

Share your experience now at
HungerNoMoreBook.com.

*"The king rejoices in your strength, LORD.
How great is his joy in the victories you give!"*
—Psalm 21:1

When we acknowledge God as our source of strength, we can take great joy during life's most positive moments. Rather than taking the credit for ourselves or blaming our success on luck, we thank the Lord for His provision. We rejoice in His strength because it is His victory.

And God's victories are certainly much better than those we could accomplish! His power is unmatched; His wisdom stands without rival. There is no army and no leader who could compete at His level. Our Lord offers everything we need to move forward in faith, a faith that rightfully returns credit to Him when accomplishments are made: "The king rejoices in your strength, LORD. How great is his joy in the victories you give!"

Share your experience now at
HungerNoMoreBook.com.

"Be exalted in your strength, LORD;
we will sing and praise your might."
—Psalm 21:13

God's strength is a reason to celebrate. Why? He is Creator of heaven and earth. The same One behind the stars in the sky is the Being we address in our own prayers. As the psalmist wrote, "Be exalted in your strength, LORD; we will sing and praise your might."

Did you ever stop to consider that God made us to remake us? He created us so we would seek Him and be transformed by Him. We were not made to stay the same, but to exalt the Lord, to sing and praise His might. Can we not pause to reflect on who He is and what He has done? He is the Lord. Let us sing and praise His name this day.

Share your experience now at
HungerNoMoreBook.com.

"In you our ancestors put their trust;
they trusted and you delivered them."
—Psalm 22:4

Noah trusted God's plan and redeemed his family and many animals from destruction. Abraham trusted God and became the leader of a great nation. Moses trusted God and led his people out of bondage. As the psalmist wrote, "In you our ancestors put their trust; they trusted and you delivered them."

This pattern of trust and deliverance extends to today. When we trust in the Lord, we often find God answering our prayers in unexpected ways. Those who have gone before us have set the example for us to follow. Let us not place our trust in our own strength; let us trust in the Lord. He has proven through our ancestors what He can do. He delivered them; He will deliver us.

Share your experience now at
HungerNoMoreBook.com.

"But you, LORD, do not be far from me.
You are my strength; come quickly to help me."
—Psalm 22:19

David's greatest fear was not how close his enemies were but how far away God was. He knew that if God showed up, his enemies did not stand a chance. But what if God didn't show up? That was the important question.

That's why David's prayer expressed, "But you, LORD, do not be far from me. You are my strength; come quickly to help me." The time was urgent; the matter was critical. What mattered was whether God would be there to answer. Should we not have the same attitude? Our fear is not about our problems, but whether God is there to answer them. The good news is that He is there. Let us turn to Him to answer our needs today.

Share your experience now at
HungerNoMoreBook.com.

FEBRUARY 19

"Future generations will be told about the Lord."
—Psalm 22:30

The best stories extend from one generation to the next. And the greatest stories of all? These are the ones God has accomplished through His people. David wrote that God's works had been so great that "future generations will be told about the Lord." The stories of the Bible have been the most translated and transmitted on the planet, reaching countless lives in every corner of the earth.

We each serve a role in communicating this story of God to future generations. Our friends, children, and grandchildren hear and see God through our lives in ways that can transform how they live in the days ahead. Let us live in such a way that future generations will be told about the Lord.

Share your experience now at
HungerNoMoreBook.com.

"The LORD is my shepherd, I lack nothing."
—Psalm 23:1

The best-known psalm opens with the words, "The LORD is my shepherd." Why a shepherd? A good shepherd both provides for the needs of his sheep yet also shows a genuine love and affection for them. David served as a shepherd in his youth and knew this role well. God had long provided for David, showing His love for him in the process.

Do we stop to recognize God's love and concern for us? Do we pause to realize the affection He has for our every need? Too often, we move through life without reflecting on God's care and provisions for us, yet we lack nothing in His presence. May David's words be our words this day: "The LORD is my shepherd, I lack nothing."

Share your experience now at
HungerNoMoreBook.com.

FEBRUARY 21

*"You prepare a table before me in the
presence of my enemies."*
—Psalm 23:5

Enemies are generally avoided. So why does David write, "You prepared a table before me in the presence of my enemies"? As a psalm of comfort, David reveals here that God can even provide peace in hostile situations. To "prepare a table" would require making peace where there is no peace.

Only God can do this. Changing the human heart is not something we can do; only the One who controls the heart can. Think of the person in your life who bothers you the most. Now imagine sitting down to enjoy a meal with this person. Seem impossible? Not with God. When necessary, He will even change those who oppose us. Let us not fear, but walk in fear of the Lord today.

Share your experience now at
HungerNoMoreBook.com.

FEBRUARY 22

"The earth is the LORD's, and everything in it."
—Psalm 24:1

Have you ever stopped to consider that everything we see belongs to God? Our possessions, our neighbor's house, even the oceans and mountains belong to Him. He owns it all.

This is why it is foolish to hold tightly to our material possessions. We do not own them, but they can own us. God has given us what we have to use for His glory, not for our own. We are to use what we have to satisfy Him, not to satisfy ourselves. Today, let us look at what we own as gifts from God to accomplish His will. As we do, we'll find ourselves clinging less and giving more. Today, let us remember: "The earth is the LORD's, and everything in it."

Share your experience now at
HungerNoMoreBook.com.

"No one who hopes in you will ever be put to shame."
—Psalm 25:3

The contrast of shame is not simply honor, but hope. David wrote, "No one who hopes in you will ever be put to shame." This contrast between hope and shame shines light on God's desire for our lives. When we reject God, we open ourselves up to shame. But if our hope is in God, we can resist shame and find strength instead.

In this psalm, shame includes the idea of defeat by an enemy. Through our Lord, we can stand confident of victory. In Him, we overcome those who oppose us through the strength of the Lord. Hardship still knocks on our door, but hope answers the door. Let us live in hope, rising above today's circumstances through the strength of our God.

Share your experience now at
HungerNoMoreBook.com.

"Show me your ways, LORD, teach me your paths."
—Psalm 25:4

One trait of a good teacher is to show rather than to tell. When it comes to God, David asks the Lord to "show me your ways, LORD, teach me your paths." This cry includes three key components for our lives today.

First, there is showing or teaching. Both words are used in parallel to express a desire to know God's will. Second, There are "your ways" or "your paths." David wants to know what God wants him to do. Third, there is the Lord, the reason for asking. Today, let us seek for God to show us His ways because of our desire to honor Him with our lives. Then let us show His ways to those we encounter in our lives.

Share your experience now at
HungerNoMoreBook.com.

FEBRUARY 25

"My eyes are ever on the LORD."
—Psalm 25:15

Eyes can be easily distracted. They blink an average of fifteen times per minute and can take in thousands of images a day. Yet the psalmist noted, "My eyes are ever on the LORD." The idea is one of complete concentration, of total attention to God and God alone.

Imagine an entire day where you only thought about God. Could you do it? Not likely. Many of us struggle to remain focused for even a few minutes. But our goal is ever-increasing emphasis on God rather than on ourselves or other pursuits. As you go about your day, seek to focus your wandering moments on God and what He has done. Let it be said of you, "My eyes are ever on the LORD."

Share your experience now at
HungerNoMoreBook.com.

69

FEBRUARY 26

"Guard my life and rescue me."
—Psalm 25:20

One of life's greatest fears is the fear of death. Like David, when life is in jeopardy, we cry out, "Guard my life and rescue me." When we are sick, we turn to a doctor. When we require surgery, we look to a surgeon. But when we face death, we turn principally to God. Why? He is the One who can guard our lives and rescue us.

Many people walk through life without considering God until they face death. Yet David walked intimately with the Lord daily. Turning to his heavenly Father when facing a life-and-death situation was not out of the ordinary because of his ongoing relationship with God. May we likewise walk with God today, as well as turning to Him during times of trouble.

Share your experience now at
HungerNoMoreBook.com.

"Test me, LORD, and try me,
examine my heart and my mind."
—Psalm 26:2

Very few invite the Lord to examine their heart. Yet David wrote, "Test me, LORD, and try me, examine my heart and mind." David walked closely with God and could confidently open himself for review. While not perfect, David's relationship with the Lord was close and vibrant, with a heart passionate to grow in faith.

Our desire must be to reach the point that we could offer God the same request. While we will never be perfect in this life, we can live closely with God, passionately growing each day. When we do, we can live with a genuine confidence, knowing we are moving forward according to the will of our heavenly Father. Our goal is to constantly improve in our walk with God.

Share your experience now at
HungerNoMoreBook.com.

"My feet stand on level ground;
in the great congregation I will praise the LORD."
—Psalm 26:12

It is one thing to praise God in private; it is another to do so among others. David makes the pledge to praise the Lord "in the great congregation," meaning among his fellow people. He was not shy or ashamed regarding his love for God. Rather, he wanted everyone to know the Lord He served.

Is this your attitude? In our culture, religion is often pushed aside as a private matter, but this is not the case for those who follow Christ. We are called to praise our God, both privately and publicly, with a longing for others to know Him as we do. Let us praise the Lord among all those we meet. Let us joyfully declare the Lord's greatness to all the world.

Share your experience now at
HungerNoMoreBook.com.

MARCH 1

"The LORD is my light and my salvation—
whom shall I fear?"
—Psalm 27:1

The contrast to fear is not merely confidence; it is the Lord. David wrote, "The LORD is my light and my salvation—whom shall I fear?" His confidence was found in God, not his own efforts. His power came from the power of the universe's Creator.

Here, the word pictures of light and salvation are used. Light served as a guide in the darkness, offering protection at night. Salvation likewise spoke of protection from enemies. Together, they communicate the appropriate contrast to fear—a deep trust in the Lord. Should you find yourself in fear today, remember David's words—"Whom shall I fear?" With the Lord, the best answer is "nothing." The Lord is our strength, our guide, and our protection. The Lord is our light and salvation.

Share your experience now at
HungerNoMoreBook.com.

*"I remain confident of this: I will see the goodness
of the LORD in the land of the living."*
—Psalm 27:13

When times are tough, it's easy to only see tough times ahead. Whether it's the economy or our family, hard times usually generate thoughts of more tough times. Yet David offers a different approach. In his words, "I remain confident of this: I will see the goodness of the LORD in the land of the living."

Despite the difficult situation that surrounded David, he anticipated a brighter future. Because of the Lord's strength, his struggle was not destined for demise but held the potential for good. This attitude is often a missing ingredient in our own spiritual lives. Today, let us live mindful that the troubles that come our way are just that—the troubles of the day. Today's struggles may be replaced with tomorrow's surprises.

Share your experience now at
HungerNoMoreBook.com.

"The LORD is the strength of his people."
—Psalm 28:8

Human strength runs down. Like a weak battery, our power turns low after only a short time. Yet the Lord's power is endless. With Him, we can move forward in strength even when our physical limitations have been exceeded. As David wrote, "The LORD is the strength of his people."

Based on this knowledge, our only restriction is how God chooses to work through our lives. We may be weak, but He is strong. We may lack the ability to move forward during life's trials, yet He knows the way. Our problems may tower over us, but God towers over our problems. Let us live today in the Lord's strength; let us live mindful that He is our power, "the strength" of His people.

Share your experience now at
HungerNoMoreBook.com.

"Ascribe to the LORD the glory due his name."
—Psalm 29:2

What does it mean to "ascribe"? A quick glance at a dictionary reveals that it means to attribute or give credit to someone. David calls his hearers to "Ascribe to the LORD the glory due his name." He knows the credit for life's blessings is not due to us, but to Someone greater—the Lord Almighty.

Too often we thank God for letting us accomplish an achievement rather than honoring Him for what He has done through us. This distinction may seem small, but it is monumental. We are the clay, not the potter. We are but a reflection that shines His light. He is the Light. Let us give glory to Him today. He is the One worthy of our praise.

Share your experience now at
HungerNoMoreBook.com.

*"LORD my God, I called to you for help,
and you healed me."*
—Psalm 30:2

Healing is a tricky business. So many deceptions have been perpetuated by faith healers and placebos that skepticism runs high. Yet healing can and does still occur in a myriad of ways. As the psalmist wrote, "LORD my God, I called to you for help, and you healed me."

In this situation, the psalmist called out for help. A human voice cried out before a healing voice responded. Even when healing does take place, it does so to fulfill a need, one beyond the human ability to correct. The one in need cried out to the One with the strength to fulfill the need. Let us reach out to Him today. Let us call to Him, and not to ourselves, as our supreme source of help.

Share your experience now at
HungerNoMoreBook.com.

MARCH 6

"Be my rock of refuge, a strong fortress to save me."
—Psalm 31:2

Our greatest need is not for a better income or a more appealing body, but for salvation. As the psalmist cries out, "Be my rock of refuge, a strong fortress to save me." In doing so, we see two parallel concepts. The first is the rock, also referred to as a strong fortress. Both terms speak concerning a place of safety.

The second concept is the refuge, or also noted as that which can "save me." We require both the act of saving and a place of safety. God provides both. When we place our trust in Him, He saves us by His grace through faith. What is the place of safety? God Himself, expressed through the Son Jesus Christ, our perfect Refuge and Salvation.

Share your experience now at
HungerNoMoreBook.com.

"Be merciful to me, LORD, for I am in distress."
—Psalm 31:9

Mercy. The very word brings to mind pictures of compassion. Feeding the hungry, housing the homeless, caring for the sick—each glimpse offers a slice of how mercy can be shown and seen in this life.

When we think of mercy, we generally think of others in need of mercy. Yet the psalmist reveals that it is often not someone else who needs God's mercy, but we ourselves. "Be merciful to me, LORD" was the cry. Why? "For I am in distress." Onlookers may see our lives and think we have life under control, but God knows our hearts. He knows when we are distressed. Let us lean on Him for mercy. Let us receive His mercy and live with mercy today.

Share your experience now at
HungerNoMoreBook.com.

"Be strong and take heart,
all you who hope in the LORD."
—Psalm 31:24

The funeral of a believer in Christ stands out as a completely different experience from those whose destiny is uncertain. When a person devoted to the Lord passes away, there is a ring of hope that transcends the grief of the moment. With God, death is the fulfillment of our eternal hope, not viewed as the end of the story.

The psalmist writes, "Be strong and take heart, all you who hope in the LORD." Those who know God can live with resilience and "take heart." Why? We have a hope that is beyond ourselves. Whether for strength in this life or looking forward to our life eternal, our future is not one of burden, but of bliss. Be strong and take heart.

Share your experience now at
HungerNoMoreBook.com.

*"Blessed is the one whose transgressions are forgiven,
whose sins are covered."*
—Psalm 32:1

When we see someone with a nice home or strong income, we often consider the person "blessed." But the psalmist depicts blessing from a different perspective–God's. Rather than the might of our possessions that defines blessing, it is forgiveness of our sins: "Blessed is the one whose transgression are forgiven, who sins are covered."

Have you thanked the Lord lately for His forgiveness of your sins? Have you forgotten the overwhelming blessing of freedom from all guilt when you came to faith in Jesus Christ? Let us not forget we are forgiven. Our sins are covered, seen no longer by our heavenly Father. We are blessed. Let us praise our God for this wondrous gift, living in newness of life today.

Share your experience now at
HungerNoMoreBook.com.

*"The LORD's unfailing love surrounds
the one who trusts in him."*
—Psalm 32:10

Some of us fear tight spaces. Whether we're in an elevator or cave, we find being surrounded as a cause for panic. Yet there is one thing that can surround us that should provide great comfort. The psalmist called it "the LORD's unfailing love." He expressed this love as something that "surrounds the one who trusts in him."

Like a warm coat on a winter day, God's love closes in around us to protect and comfort. Yet a warm coat does not stop the surrounding storm. It only protects from the elements. Likewise, our Father's love does not remove life's storms, but it does protect from them. Let us place our trust in Him. He cares for us and longs to shower us with His love.

Share your experience now at
HungerNoMoreBook.com.

*"Sing joyfully to the LORD, you righteous;
it is fitting for the upright to praise him."*
—Psalm 33:1

Praise is not only a joy for the follower of the Lord; it is the only appropriate response. "Sing joyfully to the LORD, you righteous; it is fitting for the upright to praise him." In many circles, the expression of emotion is seen as a negative or immature. Yet this verse injects passion into the scenario. We are called to sing, and to sing "joyfully."

To do so requires more than a movement of the mouth; it requires a movement of the heart. Our praise must extend beyond the words on a page or screen to a connection between Father and child, Creator and the created. Let joy exude from your soul as you worship Him today. It is fitting. Let us praise Him.

Share your experience now at
HungerNoMoreBook.com.

"By the word of the LORD the heavens were made."
—Psalm 33:6

Scholars debate the how of the universe's creation, but there is no doubt who created it: "By the word of the LORD the heavens were made." Without a Creator, there would be no creation. Without the Word, there would be no world. Without our heavenly Father, there would be no heavens.

Throughout Scripture, the focus regarding creation appears to center on who made it all rather than how it was made. We have been given some clues, yet not the details of the universe's design. Maybe this was so we would concentrate our attention on the Creator rather than the creation. When He is savored, the rest is secondary. Let us praise our Creator today. Let us give our attention to the word of the Lord.

Share your experience now at
HungerNoMoreBook.com.

March 13

"The eyes of the LORD are on those who fear him."
—Psalm 33:18

God is not a man with a body like ours. When Scripture tells us "the eyes of the LORD are on those who fear him," we are simply provided a picture of an important truth: God seeks God-worshippers. He's on the lookout and longs for those who devote their lives to Him. When we do, His attention is on us.

Of course, God sees us no matter who we are or what we do. Yet there is a special sense in which God honors those who honor Him. Scripture abounds with examples of men and women whose lives were transformed by the Lord. These were the same men and women who lived by faith in Him. This is no coincidence. God is paying attention to our lives. Are we?

Share your experience now at
HungerNoMoreBook.com.

MARCH 14

"We wait in hope for the LORD;
he is our help and our shield."
—Psalm 33:20

One thing we tend to despise is waiting. A long line, long traffic, or a long wait on the phone is often all that is needed to ruin our day. Yet the psalmist reveals a situation in which waiting is a positive: "We wait in hope for the LORD; he is our help and our shield."

When we wait in line, the end of the experience is uncertain. With God, our wait will result in His answer, an answer that is always perfect. We may not enjoy the wait, but it can serve as part of God's plan for our lives in a way only He knows. Let us not grumble or despise waiting on our Lord. He has good in store for those who wait.

Share your experience now at
HungerNoMoreBook.com.

"I will extol the LORD at all times;
his praise will always be on my lips."
—Psalm 34:1

It is easy to praise God when life goes smoothly, but what about when it doesn't? Do we praise Him anyway? The psalmist makes clear, "I will extol the LORD at all times; his praise will always be on my lips." The words "at all times" and "always" make clear that our constant focus must be on praising God despite our circumstances.

Like a marathon runner, the athlete often does not want to run the marathon; he or she wants to be finished with the long race. Yet the process is required to enjoy the accomplishment. In our worship, we must often begin praising God before we begin to enjoy His presence. Praise Him today regardless of circumstances. Let His praise always be on our lips.

Share your experience now at
HungerNoMoreBook.com.

"Taste and see that the LORD is good;
blessed is the one who takes refuge in him."
—Psalm 34:8

One of the most powerful advertisements for a new food is a free sample. When we try out a new item, we may find that we like it and then purchase more. In a similar way, we are encouraged to "Taste and see that the LORD is good."

When we share our faith with others, this "taste and see" approach can also serve us well. Rather than seeking to "convert" someone, we can begin by asking the person to "taste and see." When people truly experience a glimpse of how Jesus can change their lives, it is often all that is necessary to convince them to become His followers. Let us help others to taste and see that the Lord is good today.

Share your experience now at
HungerNoMoreBook.com.

*"The eyes of the LORD are on the righteous,
and his ears are attentive to their cry."*
—Psalm 34:15

Eyes and ears represent two of our key senses used to understand the world around us. Likewise, "The eyes of the LORD are on the righteous, and his ears are attentive to their cry." His eyes and ears are, in a spiritual sense, used to understand His people.

These words are written to reveal that God gives attention to our needs. His focus is "on the righteous" and "to their cry." God is not far off, apart from our hurts and pains. He is with us through the trials of life. In fact, He is with us and eager to help with our frustrations and difficulties. Though we cannot see Him, He is there. Let us turn to Him with our cries today.

Share your experience now at
HungerNoMoreBook.com.

"The LORD is close to the brokenhearted and saves those who are crushed in spirit."
—Psalm 34:18

Where is God when life falls apart? Close. According to the psalmist, "The LORD is close to the brokenhearted." Why? Not for our doom, but because he "saves those who are crushed in spirit." God can be found close when we feel crushed. He is not only there, but He cares. He longs to help our spirit by the power of His Spirit.

Throughout history, the Lord has shown special endearment for those in difficult situations—widows, the fatherless, the poor, immigrants, the sick, the disabled, the elderly, those grieving lost loved ones, and many others. And still today, He remains close. He is there to help. Let us not question whether God is there; let us praise Him that He is.

Share your experience now at
HungerNoMoreBook.com.

MARCH 19

"The righteous person may have many troubles, but the LORD delivers him from them all."
—Psalm 34:19

Following God does not equal an easy life. In fact, those who have walked closely with God throughout history have often endured the worst suffering. Joseph was a slave. David was a wanted man. The disciples died for their faith in Christ. As the psalmist wrote, "The righteous person may have many troubles."

Thankfully, this is not the end of the story. Those who follow the Lord may experience difficulty, "but the LORD delivers him from them all." In the midst of our trials, God provides answers. We are given a difficult journey, but we are also given an all-powerful Guide to lead and to help us. Let us not see today's troubles as a reason to give up; let us see them as an opportunity for God to deliver.

Share your experience now at
HungerNoMoreBook.com.

MARCH 20

"The LORD will rescue his servants."
—Psalm 34:22

Every great story includes a hero who longs to rescue those in peril. Whether it is a knight saving a princess or a teacher rescuing a class of under-resourced kids, there is always a hero, those who need a hero, and a rescue.

The same is true in the grand story revealed by God. In this account, He is the Hero. We are the ones in peril. According to the psalmist, "The LORD will rescue his servants." The tension, as in any good story, is that we don't always feel like God is on His way to save us. We often think we are far from God or that the problems of life will win. Yet our Hero is there. He will rescue His servants.

Share your experience now at
HungerNoMoreBook.com.

"Take up shield and armor;
arise and come to my aid."
—Psalm 35:2

We often speak of God as our Father or our Master, but rarely as our Warrior. Yet David makes clear: "Take up shield and armor; arise and come to my aid." This war veteran knew the value of a fellow warrior arrayed in shield and armor fighting at his side. Through many battles, such men had helped to spare David's life from certain death.

With this background in mind, David expresses his desire for God to show up like a warrior dressed for battle. David faced certain demise. Without God's intervention, David could not succeed. He needed help. He needed the Lord, in full armor and weapons, to save the day. God can conquer the spiritual foes we face. Let us count on our Warrior to save.

Share your experience now at
HungerNoMoreBook.com.

MARCH 22

"How long, Lord, will you look on?"
—Psalm 35:17

One of the most frustrating experiences of life is when those who oppose God prosper. In fact, it's even worse when such people prosper and those of us who follow God struggle. We begin to wonder if our Lord somehow has His schedule of blessings mixed up. You think to yourself, *God, are You sure that wasn't supposed to be my blessing?*

The Psalms often reflect on this same frustration. David noted, "How long, Lord, will You look on?" He grew tired of God's apparent lack of response to his situation while the wicked continued to succeed. Yet God has not forgotten us. His schedule is different from ours, yet much better. He will answer at just the right time, offering His strength to meet our needs.

Share your experience now at
HungerNoMoreBook.com.

*"My tongue will proclaim your righteousness,
your praises all day long."*
—Psalm 35:28

There is no end to praising God. We are called to praise Him now. Some day we will praise Him for eternity. Recognizing this, David wrote, "My tongue will proclaim your righteousness, your praises all day long." We can worship God forever because His greatness is unending.

Realize this: Even if we praised God for all of the good things He has done in our lives up to this point, we could start now and not run out of blessings to list during this lifetime. One day, we'll see God for who He is, sparking an eternal response of worship. Let us not settle with a quick thank-You today. Let us honor Him throughout our waking moments. Let us praise Him "all day long."

Share your experience now at
HungerNoMoreBook.com.

"Your love, LORD, reaches to the heavens,
your faithfulness to the skies."
—Psalm 36:5

God's love cannot be measured. When David speaks of God's love, he declared that it reached to the heavens and that the Lord's faithfulness stretched to the skies. This poetic imagery simply reinforces the idea that our heavenly Father's love is beyond measure and surpasses our ability to comprehend.

Yet many people still struggle with whether God loves them. Perhaps you do as well. Know for certain that God's immeasurable love includes an infinite love for you. He knows everything about you. He created you. He watches over you even now. Do not doubt His love for you. Embrace it. Enjoy it. You may not be able to measure God's love, but you can certainly experience it. Remember God's perfect love for you today.

Share your experience now at
HungerNoMoreBook.com.

MARCH 25

"How priceless is your unfailing love, O God!
People take refuge in the shadow of your wings."
—Psalm 36:7

God's love is not only beyond measure; it is also beyond price. The psalmist notes, "How priceless is your unfailing love, O God! People take refuge in the shadow of your wings." As a mother bird protects her infant birds under her wings, God keeps us close to His side, making clear His love and protection for us.

As a result, His love is called "unfailing." God is perfect and cannot fail. Neither can His love. We can cling to Him and stay close to Him, knowing He will protect us, no matter the situation. It is not the size of our problems but the size of our God that matters most. He loves us and will protect us through all of today's struggles.

Share your experience now at
HungerNoMoreBook.com.

March 26

"Take delight in the LORD,
and he will give you the desires of your heart."
—Psalm 37:4

What did God mean when He inspired the words, "Take delight in the LORD, and he will give you the desires of your heart"? Does this mean if we please God, He'll give us whatever we want? Not exactly. There is a direct correlation between our godly delight and our human desire. When we walk closely with God, we increasingly long for what He wants rather than what we want.

It means those who find their joy in God will crave what God wants done. If you find yourself desiring the things of this world, the corrective is to delight in the Lord. Devote yourself to Him. He will give you the desires of your heart, a heart that longs for the longings of God.

Share your experience now at
HungerNoMoreBook.com.

"Be still before the LORD and wait patiently for him."
—Psalm 37:7

To "be still" is much more difficult than it sounds. To "be still" means to stop moving or to stop striving, activities we often view as the answer to our problems. Yet God's way is often to stop rather than to strive: "Be still before the LORD and wait patiently for him."

This verse does not remove the need for human effort; it removes our unhealthy emphasis on it. There is a time to work and a time to wait, a time to strive and a time to be still. Perhaps it has been some time since you have paused to "wait patiently for him." If so, let today be the day you reflect in this moment to hear what God desires to communicate to you.

Share your experience now at
HungerNoMoreBook.com.

March 28

"The meek will inherit the land and enjoy peace and prosperity."
—Psalm 37:11

We often associate "meek" with "weak." Yet God contrasts the meek with those who do evil. Those who are meek are the ones who walk humbly and obediently with God. David notes, "The meek will inherit the land and enjoy peace and prosperity."

The emphasis here is not on health and wealth, but rather upon blessings to those who live according to God's ways. The wicked may appear to prosper, but their gain will eventually vanish. Their apparent successes will not last. Those who serve the Lord will ultimately be those who succeed spiritually, both now and in eternity. Let us not settle for what this world calls success; let us seek to be "meek" and please our heavenly Father.

Share your experience now at
HungerNoMoreBook.com.

*"Better the little that the righteous have
than the wealth of many wicked"*
—Psalm 37:16

Many of our prayer requests focus on financial matters. Yet David notes, "Better the little that the righteous have than the wealth of many wicked." Despite any lack of financial wealth, we are more blessed than we realize. What matters most to God is not our net worth but our eternal worth.

While financial concerns are an important and necessary part of life, they must not take priority over our relationship with God. He seeks our faithfulness more than our financial prosperity. When He receives central focus, He can trust that our monetary resources will be used in a way that honors His will. Regardless of what we have, let us honor God with our lives. Righteousness is far more valuable than financial wealth.

Share your experience now at
HungerNoMoreBook.com.

"The righteous give generously."
—Psalm 37:21

Righteousness and generosity stand inseparable. The person whose heart longs for God also longs to give to others. The one who longs to give to others also longs for God: "the righteous give generously."

The emphasis in Scripture is not the amount we give, but the attitude with which we give. Whether we live in poverty or prosperity, we can still live generously. Generosity is a matter of integrity, not money. We may not enjoy speaking of finances when it comes to our spiritual lives, yet it is clear that our handling of money reflects our heart for God and for others. Let us ask God this day how we can please Him with how we use our God-given resources.

Share your experience now at
HungerNoMoreBook.com.

March 31

"The LORD makes firm the steps
of the one who delights in him."
—Psalm 37:23

God not only desires our obedience; He desires that we delight in Him: "The LORD makes firm the steps of the one who delights in him." Those who do are given sure footing, protection from slipping away from the path God seeks. In our delight for God, we find a focus that pulls us forward and away from harm.

Our central question this day must be, "Do I delight in God?" If not, why not? If not, what needs to change so that we do? Do not let this day pass without taking the time to address this all-important question. Pursue God and call out to Him until your clear response is, "Yes, I delight in God. He will make my steps firm."

Share your experience now at
HungerNoMoreBook.com.

April 1

"I have never seen the righteous forsaken."
—Psalm 37:25

The righteous are those who follow the will of God. According to the psalmist, "I have never seen the righteous forsaken." Those who live for God may struggle or suffer greatly, yet God is always there. He is always by our side, offering His love and protection for our every need.

We may think God has forgotten us at times, but He has not. We may not feel God is close to us at times, but He is. Our emotions often betray the reality that God is there, that He loves us every moment of every day, guiding us along our daily journey. Let us cling to His words today: "I have never seen the righteous forsaken." He will never leave us.

Share your experience now at
HungerNoMoreBook.com.

APRIL 2

"The mouths of the righteous utter wisdom,
and their tongues speak what is just."
—Psalm 37:30

The mouth is the body's most powerful weapon. With it we can praise God or curse Him, we can encourage or discourage. The psalmist observes that the "mouths of the righteous utter wisdom, and their tongues speak what is just." If we wish to live righteous in our walk with the Lord, speaking wisdom is a critical component.

Yet when we seek to review our words from the past day, how many of them were speaking truth or building up others? Too often, we are quick to criticize and complain rather than to encourage or praise. Today, let us begin anew our attempt to honor God with our words. Let's seek to communicate God's truth with God's love. Let our tongues speak what is just.

Share your experience now at
HungerNoMoreBook.com.

"A future awaits those who seek peace."
—Psalm 37:37

God loves those who seek peace. In fact, we are told, "A future awaits those who seek peace." What kind of future does the psalmist have in mind? A salvation to anticipate rather than judgment; a hope of eternity with God rather than eternity apart from Him.

The question is: How do we seek peace? Peace begins with a choice. When we choose to pursue peace with God and others, we start the process that brings change to life's situations. We may not be able to control how others react, but we can determine to live in a way that reflects God's desires as much as possible. Such actions merely anticipate the eternal peace God's people will experience permanently some day in heaven. There our perfect "future awaits."

Share your experience now at
HungerNoMoreBook.com.

APRIL 4

*"LORD, do not rebuke me in your anger
or discipline me in your wrath."*
—Psalm 38:1

We live as fallen, imperfect people. On many occasions, we have deserved the wrath of God rather than His forgiveness. Yet He has extended His grace. The psalmist understood this divine attribute, asking God, "LORD, do not rebuke me in your anger or discipline me in your wrath."

This request was not to seek a license to sin, but to receive forgiveness. The psalmist knew discipline was deserved, yet also knew God is compassionate and full of love. When we fail our Lord, we likewise ask for His grace, knowing we do not deserve it, but that He continues to provide it. Without Him we would be doomed; with Him we are renewed. He is the difference, the One who cleanses us from all unrighteousness.

Share your experience now at
HungerNoMoreBook.com.

APRIL 5

"All my longings lie open before you, Lord."
—Psalm 38:9

We cannot hide from God. He knows our actions, our words, and our thoughts. This is why the psalmist could pen, "All my longings lie open before you, Lord." There is no use to pretend. Our Lord has supreme understanding of every facet of our being.

Such a realization is at once both frightening and fascinating. It is frightening in the sense that we stand before God's perfect judgment. It is fascinating in the sense that God loves us enough to track our every detail. Let us look to Him with a heart filled with reverence. He is the perfect, all-knowing Creator who loves us despite our frailty. Since all of our longings lie open before Him, let us seek to long for Him.

Share your experience now at
HungerNoMoreBook.com.

"LORD, do not forsake me;
do not be far from me, my God."
–Psalm 38:21

David's greatest fear was not the loss of his life, but the loss of his God. He cried out, "LORD, do not forsake me; do not be far from me, my God." David longed to be with God and near Him. Nothing else mattered more.

Do we live with the same passion for the Lord's presence? How much would we miss His Spirit if He were to suddenly vanish? If we could live a second without noticing His disappearance from our lives, we have space to grow closer to God. Let us seek for our passion to match that of David in this regard. Let us likewise call out, "Lord, do not forsake me; do not be far from me, my God."

Share your experience now at
HungerNoMoreBook.com.

APRIL 7

"Show me, LORD, my life's end and the number of my days; let me know how fleeting my life is."
—Psalm 39:4

This life is but a breath. Like the morning dew, it dissipates without warning. Like the blink of an eye, our lives in this world open and shut in a flash. David sensed this fleeting existence and wrote, "Show me, LORD, my life's end and the number of my days." He wanted to understand what time he had left so he would live in a way that honored God.

We do not know if he had just attended a funeral or faced death himself, but we can resonate with his request. When we understand the shortness of life, we live life differently. Let us live this day dedicated to the Creator of life, knowing we will one day experience eternity with Him.

Share your experience now at
HungerNoMoreBook.com.

"But now, Lord, what do I look for?
My hope is in you."
—Psalm 39:7

The competing desires of life can often satisfy for a moment, but quickly fade. Whether money, relationships, success, or fame—each leaves the soul unsettled. What is the answer? David answered in the form of a question: "But now, Lord, what do I look for? My hope is in you."

David realized what we discover along life's journey: there is no adequate substitute for God. Our search for hope will continue until we find our journey's end at the feet of our Lord. In Him is our hope. In Him is our satisfaction. We need not live in doubt, but rather in faith. Let us live mindful of His perfection today. Let us focus on the hope found only in our God.

Share your experience now at
HungerNoMoreBook.com.

"I waited patiently for the LORD;
he turned to me and heard my cry."
—Psalm 40:1

Waiting is active, not passive. We are called to wait "patiently for the LORD." This pattern marked the biblical patriarchs, from Noah's days on the ark to Abraham's diligent wait for a son to fulfill God's promise. These men and many others show that waiting can be as difficult or even more difficult than acting in our own strength.

When we do wait patiently, we experience the same result as David: "He turned to me and heard my cry." God does not cause us to wait simply for the sake of waiting. He responds to our needs with His perfect intervention at the appropriate time. We cry out...and wait. He hears...and responds. Let us call out—and wait patiently—for the Lord today.

Share your experience now at
HungerNoMoreBook.com.

APRIL 10

"None can compare with you; were I to speak and tell of your deeds, they would be too many to declare."
—Psalm 40:5

God has no equal. Just His known works are beyond retelling. As David sang, "None can compare with you; were I to speak and tell of your deeds, they would be too many to declare." Our Lord's acts are beyond comparison and beyond number.

When we consider what He has done in our own lives, our souls echo David's thought. We quickly lose track of the many ways God has blessed our lives, changed our circumstances, and shown Himself faithful. Yet He has had these actions prepared for our lives since before the world's foundation. What a powerful Father! God's countless works are worthy of our endless praise. Let us remember His goodness and speak of His mighty works today.

Share your experience now at
HungerNoMoreBook.com.

APRIL 11

"I desire to do your will, my God."
—Psalm 40:8

We often claim we want to do God's will, but do we truly desire His plans for the details of our lives? David sang, "I desire to do your will, my God." His close connection with "my God" compelled David to long for God's control over every area of his life.

When we say, "Your will be done," we indicate two choices. First, we declare God's agenda takes top priority. Second, we express that our own desires must conform to the Lord's plans rather than our own. As John the Baptist would answer regarding Jesus, "He must increase; I must decrease." May we likewise choose to "decrease" in comparison to Christ's plan for our lives. Let us pursue God's will throughout the moments of our day.

Share your experience now at
HungerNoMoreBook.com.

*"Do not withhold your mercy from me, LORD;
may your love and faithfulness always protect me."*
—Psalm 40:11

God's love is our greatest protection. No weapon can conquer love; no power can thwart its impact. Perhaps this is why David's longing was, "Do not withhold your mercy from me, LORD; may your love and faithfulness always protect me."

Whether through his struggles against the elements and wildlife as a shepherd or in his flight from Saul and his army, David relied on the Lord to rescue. The same strength that carried David through sleepless nights in fields and caves was the same force he sought in this moment. When we are at our weakest, God's love carries us through. The same love that raised our Savior from the grave works in us. Let us rely on the protection of His love through today's struggles.

Share your experience now at
HungerNoMoreBook.com.

*"Blessed are those who have regard for the weak; the
LORD delivers them in times of trouble."*
—Psalm 41:1

David's Psalm reveals a key focus for those who wish to be blessed—caring for the weak. Rather than a focus on personal strength or prosperity, God's highest concern concentrates on those without. In David's words, "Blessed are those who have regard for the weak; the LORD delivers them in times of trouble."

God has chosen to help those in their weakness who care for others in their weakness. Even the example of His Son Jesus Christ unveils a life of One willing to lay down His life on behalf of the weaknesses of others. If caring for those in need, we follow His path as well as create a path of love that points toward our God. He will show Himself strong and deliver.

Share your experience now at
HungerNoMoreBook.com.

"As the deer pants for streams of water, so my soul pants for you, my God."
—Psalm 42:1

In the desolate wilderness of Judea, a deer might travel a great distance from one source of water to the next. The result? Panting. The animal's body could be heaving in the pursuit of even a small stream to quench its thirst.

The psalmist uses this illustration to express his own desire for the Lord: "As the deer pants for streams of water, so my soul pants for you, my God." This was more than a passion; it was a life-and-death situation. His soul would wither up without God to answer his need. God's presence was absolutely essential to sustaining life. Do we desire God with such zeal? This is to be our goal. We must not simply desire God; we must live in total dependence.

Share your experience now at
HungerNoMoreBook.com.

APRIL 15

*"By day the LORD directs his love, at night his song
is with me—a prayer to the God of my life."*
—Psalm 42:8

God's love is never on holiday. Whether early morning, noon, or deep into the night, His affection pursues and sustains us. As the psalmist observed, "By day the LORD directs his love, at night his song is with me." The continuum of day and night encompass the entirety of our existence.

When we do not sense God's love in our lives, it is not because He has left but often due to our failure to recognize His presence. Even in the greatest of suffering, our Lord is by our side. We may question His ways, but we dare never question His love. Every moment of every day, His love remains faithful, dependable, and able to comfort us in our times of need.

Share your experience now at
HungerNoMoreBook.com.

"Put your hope in God, for I will yet praise him,
my Savior and my God."
—Psalm 43:5

When life takes an unexpected turn, we tend to stop praising God and begin questioning Him. The psalmist takes a different approach. During times of testing, he declares, "Put your hope in God, for I will yet praise him, my Savior and my God."

Asking questions is not wrong; failing to worship God is. Whether in times of doubt, tragedy, loneliness, sickness, or pain, our goal must be to say, "I will yet praise him." If He is our Savior, He is mighty to save. If He is our God, He controls all that takes place. We are called to honor Him regardless of our emotions or circumstances, knowing He is good and that His hope endures through all situations.

Share your experience now at
HungerNoMoreBook.com.

*"In God we make our boast all day long,
and we will praise your name forever."*
—Psalm 44:8

Is it bad to boast about God? Not according to the psalmist. He wrote, "In God we make our boast all day long, and we will praise your name forever." He not only encouraged boasting about the Lord, but doing so all day!

Often, our goal is to not be ashamed of God or the gospel of Jesus Christ, following the command of the apostle Paul in Romans 1:16. Yet in our worship of God, we can both praise and boast of how great God is and the things He has done. If we will declare His greatness for eternity why not begin now by expressing His unsurpassing worth in our times of worship. Let us say, "How great is our God!"

Share your experience now at
HungerNoMoreBook.com.

"You have rejected and humbled us."
—Psalm 44:9

When the nation of Israel rejected God, the Lord allowed opposing nations to overcome it. Despite the miraculous signs accomplished in the past, the present situation looked as if God had left them. In the psalmist's words, "You have rejected and humbled us."

Do you ever feel like God has rejected you? When our health or our relationships fail us, it's easy to pass the blame and suggest that God has failed. Yet just as God still had a plan for the people of Israel, God has a plan for us even during failure. His goal is to draw us near to Him and reveal His glory. Let us not turn against God when it feels He has left; let us turn to Him.

Share your experience now at
HungerNoMoreBook.com.

"Rise up and help us;
rescue us because of your unfailing love."
—Psalm 44:26

Why should we ask God to help us? We certainly have our personal interests at stake, yet the psalmist utilized a different approach to call upon the Lord's help. He urged the Father to "rise up and help us; rescue us because of your unfailing love."

Rather than a focus on his own need, the psalmist appealed to God's attribute of unfailing love as a reason for intervention. A great lesson can be found in these words for our own prayer lives. We don't simply come to our Lord asking for "me." We also appeal to His greatness. When we do, we remind both God and ourselves that our help is based on who He is—our God of unfailing love.

Share your experience now at
HungerNoMoreBook.com.

*"My heart is stirred by a noble theme
as I recite my verses for the king."*
—Psalm 45:1

Weddings are a time of celebration. In a song composed for wedding celebration, the psalmist noted, "My heart is stirred by a noble theme as I recite my verses for the king." Singing words of encouragement to the groom, bride, and their future children, we find an embrace of marriage and family from God's perspective—one of great value, joy, and love.

In a world in which marriage is often redefined or poorly experienced, our attitude toward family can easily become jaded. Yet God's view of the institution He created informs our attitude today. When we think of our family, our spouse, parents, or children, let us see them as a gift from God—and a reason to celebrate.

Share your experience now at
HungerNoMoreBook.com.

"Your throne, O God, will last for ever and ever; a scepter of justice will be the scepter of your kingdom."
—Psalm 45:6

Growing up, many of us realized that life is not fair. The bully gets away with everything. Some kids could ace a test without trying while others failed despite much study. Our sense of right and wrong stood acutely aware that injustices were taking place, often with little we could do to change the situation.

Yet there is a day in which the world will be just. When the Lord reigns, the psalmist notes, "A scepter of justice will be the scepter of your kingdom." When His kingdom comes, life will be fair; justice will be served. This life will continue to treat us unfairly at times, but there will be a future secure from such injustice. Let us rejoice in anticipation of God's future kingdom.

Share your experience now at
HungerNoMoreBook.com.

"I will perpetuate your memory through all generations; therefore the nations will praise you for ever and ever."
—Psalm 45:17

Do you realize that how we live for God now influences eternity? Every moment of every day, our seemingly unimportant actions have the potential to change the course of life among entire nations. Small actions done with great passion have the potential to transform the world.

The psalmist shared, "I will perpetuate your memory through all generations; therefore the nations will praise you forever and ever." Because of this writer's declaration of God's greatness, others would hear of God and worship. The ultimate result would be that nations would praise God. Do not underestimate the value of today's actions. What you do could have an impact on eternity. Let your life share His love today. May nations give praise to God as a result of your commitment to the Lord.

Share your experience now at
HungerNoMoreBook.com.

"God is our refuge and strength,
an ever-present help in trouble."
—Psalm 46:1

God is always with us. He is with us every single moment of our lives. The psalmist called our Lord "an ever-present help in trouble." During difficult times, God's presence serves as a strong reminder of His faithfulness with us through all situations.

Even the best human relationships let us down. Patience wears thin, arguments take place, friends move away, and loved ones pass away. But not God. "Ever-present" emphasizes His eternal togetherness with us. The God who created us will never leave. He is our refuge; He is our strength. Let us not rely on our own power to sustain our day; let us count on the One who is with us in our time of trouble. He is our ever-present help.

Share your experience now at
HungerNoMoreBook.com.

*"The LORD Almighty is with us;
the God of Jacob is our fortress."*
—Psalm 46:7

The Bible often refers to the Lord as the God of Jacob. This reference directs us to the son of Isaac and grandson of Abraham found in Scripture's opening book of Genesis. Despite Jacob's deceptions, God chose Jacob as the one who would become the father of twelve sons who would later become the twelve tribes of Israel. The God of Jacob was not only Jacob's God, but also the God of his family and of the Jewish nation.

When people look at your life, do they see the Lord as your God, the God of Jill or the God of Roger? Despite our failures, God has called us to lives marked by our worship of Him. Let others see God as the One we follow.

Share your experience now at
HungerNoMoreBook.com.

"Come and see what the LORD has done."
—Psalm 46:8

Invitation is a strong influence. When we are invited to a party, we feel special; our participation matters. When invited to a wedding, we have a sense of connectedness to those involved. The same is true when we invite others to experience what God is doing in our lives. When we ask someone to "Come and see what the LORD has done," that person feel as if their involvement means something.

Is there someone we could invite into our lives to share God's goodness? Whether a close friend or a new one, there are those around us who need an encouraging word. When they experience the stories of God's grace through your life, they are both lifted up and pointed to the Savior we praise.

Share your experience now at
HungerNoMoreBook.com.

"Be still, and know that I am God."
—Psalm 46:10

Many times, to "be still" is one of the most difficult requests that can be made upon our lives. We crave action, interaction, and stimulation of all kinds. To stop reveals pain. To pause requires thinking of those we have hurt, regrets in our relationships, or times of suppressed grief from the passing of a loved one.

But God does not ask us to "be still" to cause us pain. He knows when we run ahead in our own strength we often mistake His power for our own. We must frequently be still, not to remind ourselves of our weaknesses, but to remind ourselves of God's greatness. Then we recognize He is God. We are not. His strength is the source of our strength.

Share your experience now at
HungerNoMoreBook.com.

*"For the LORD Most High is awesome,
the great King over all the earth."*
—Psalm 47:2

We believe God is good, but awesome? Many times, our lives do not reflect such an attitude. Yet the psalmist wrote, "For the LORD Most High is awesome, the great King over all the earth." Awesome is a term reserved for the highest of a particular category. Here the psalmist notes God is the great King; He reigns over the entire planet.

Our view of God determines how we live for Him. How do we move from "God is good" to "God is awesome"? First, we reflect on what He has already done. Second, we spend time worshiping Him. When we do these two things consistently, we will find ourselves declaring as the psalmist did that "the LORD Most High is awesome."

Share your experience now at
HungerNoMoreBook.com.

*"God is the King of all the earth;
sing to him a psalm of praise."*
—Psalm 47:7

A nation's leader wields much power. Whether president, prime minister, or king, those who lead hold great influence. As such, they demand our respect. But no one has the power of God. He is King of all the earth. According to the psalmist, the appropriate response is to "sing to him a psalm of praise."

With God, we not only show honor; we shower praise. We hum, sing, and orchestrate worship designed to express our love for Him. No single song is enough. Hundreds of psalms could not adequately complete the task. Only an eternity of worship in God's presence will appropriately declare the greatness of our King. Today let us not settle simply knowing God is great. Let us sing praise to His name.

Share your experience now at
HungerNoMoreBook.com.

*"Great is the LORD, and most worthy of praise,
in the city of our God, his holy mountain."*
—Psalm 48:1

Even to this day, the Jewish people do not say the Lord's Name when reading Scripture. The sacred name of God is so holy that a second term, Adonai, is used instead. The greatest of reverence is given to the One who deserves it. His name is holy.

This attitude of reverence may explain in part the many glorious titles used in relation to God's name in the Psalms. The psalmist called Him "most worthy of praise" to indicate there was no one else who should receive as much attention or honor. God is not only a friend or our leader—He is holy. He is to be revered. He is worthy of all praise. Let us live giving Him the honor due His name.

Share your experience now at
HungerNoMoreBook.com.

*"Like your name, O God, your praise reaches
to the ends of the earth."*
—Psalm 48:10

The phrase "the ends of the earth" is often used in Scripture to indicate the idea of "everywhere." In Psalm 48, we are told God's "praise reaches to the ends of the earth." The idea is one of God's people praising God everywhere at all times regardless of location or situation.

In our hypermobile culture, we often exchange messages or work with people across the country and around the world. As we do, let us be mindful of how to express praise to God that extends to everywhere God allows us to reach. Let us share His greatness and love with all we can wherever we can and whenever we can. Let us be part of His praise reaching to the ends of the earth.

Share your experience now at
HungerNoMoreBook.com.

May 1

"For this God is our God for ever and ever;
he will be our guide even to the end."
—Psalm 48:14

Some people get into religion for a brief period of time, then depart. Not so with those who know God. For them, "This God is our God for ever and ever; he will be our guide even to the end." Those who follow the Lord do not commit for a season, but for all time. If there is one God from all eternity, then we are to worship this one God for all eternity. Nothing else satisfies, nothing else substitutes.

Perhaps your love for God has grown cold or taken a turn from its original passion. If so, let today be the day this ends. There is one God and we have but one life to offer Him. Let us worship Him with full devotion today.

Share your experience now at
HungerNoMoreBook.com.

"God will redeem me from the realm of the dead;
he will surely take me to himself."
—Psalm 49:15

This life is not all there is. In fact, this life is but a speck in comparison with the length of eternity. Beyond our final breath in this life is life everlasting. It will be spent either with God forever or apart from Him forever. The difference is whether trust in His Son Jesus Christ as our Savior.

Those who know the Lord can confidently say, "God will redeem me from the realm of the dead; he will surely take me to himself." We can look to the future without anxiety and with full confidence that we will forever be "with Him." No matter our problems today, our anticipation of eternity gives us a joy that can carry us through our temporary struggles.

Share your experience now at
HungerNoMoreBook.com.

"Do not be overawed when others grow rich,
when the splendor of their houses increases."
—Psalm 49:16

When we see others accumulate vast wealth, our initial reaction is to be impressed. "Look at what this person has!" But this is not the response God desires. The psalmist wrote, "Do not be overawed when others grow rich, when the splendor of their houses increases." Why not? Riches are external and temporary. God looks at the internal and eternal.

Our Lord desires a heart that longs for Him rather than one easily impressed by possessions. He offers eternal riches that far surpass the wealth of this world. When we value riches above a godly life, we place ourselves before our Father's will. When we value God above all, we value what matters most. Let us live thankful for what He has already given us.

Share your experience now at
HungerNoMoreBook.com.

"He is a God of justice."
—Psalm 50:6

Today's courts seek to serve justice, yet often fall short. No human system can adequately address the problems of our world. Only God can provide perfect justice, for "He is a God of justice." His nature includes making things right, transcending our moral sense of good and evil with His perfect moral nature.

This same longing for justice has been placed within each of our hearts. We may not have the ability to change all of the world's wrongs, but we can make a difference where we are. Let us help stand for what is right and to help those in need as we are able until the day the God of justice returns to right every wrong and provide perfect justice.

Share your experience now at
HungerNoMoreBook.com.

"Every animal of the forest is mine,
and the cattle on a thousand hills."
—Psalm 50:10

God is never bankrupt. He owns every animal of every forest and every farm. "Every animal of the forest is mine, and the cattle on a thousand hills." Our Lord's riches are without limit and without equal.

There is a blessing in this truth for those of us who follow Him. Since God owns everything, He can provide for our every need according to His perfect will. This does not mean He will make us rich or prosperous in this life, but He has the ability to meet our needs perfectly. We need not fear when we lack resources in this life. Rather, we cry out to the One who controls every resource, asking His solution to our situations and limitations.

Share your experience now at
HungerNoMoreBook.com.

MAY 6

"Call on me in the day of trouble; I will deliver you."
—Psalm 50:15

God delivers. His one request? "Call on me in the day of trouble; I will deliver you." Our Lord desires to hear from us and to respond to our needs.

Many times we are taught, "God helps those who help themselves." Some even believe these words are found in the Bible, though they are not. God does not ask us to work so He can bless us. He asks us to call to Him so He can deliver us. We are not working interdependently with God, though we can cooperate with Him. Yet, we are fully dependent on Him for solutions to life's problems. Only when He answers can we rest assured our needs will be met. He is the One who delivers. We are the ones who call out.

Share your experience now at
HungerNoMoreBook.com.

May 7

"Consider this, you who forget God."
—Psalm 50:22

It is a sin to forget God. In fact, many of the Psalms focus our attention on remembering the great things the Lord has done in our lives. When we forget God, we no longer praise Him. When we fail to remember His goodness, we begin to trust in our own goodness. The end result is selfish living that dishonors God and others.

If we wish to please the Lord, we must first remember Him. When we reflect on His greatness, we find our joy renewed. When we meditate on what He has done, we live with great anticipation regarding what He will do. Remembering God is respecting God. Let us live mindful of Him today; let us not forget the Lord.

Share your experience now at
HungerNoMoreBook.com.

*"Have mercy on me, O God,
according to your unfailing love."*
—Psalm 51:1

When we have sinned against God, the only solution is His mercy. David was called a man after God's own heart, yet when he sinned by taking another man's wife, he could only throw himself upon God's mercy. His status as king was insufficient; only the mercy of the King of kings could suffice. "Have mercy on me, O God, according to your unfailing love."

If this is true of King David, what does it say for our lives? When we fall to temptation, our response must be one of repentance. Excuses, apathy, or secrets only delay our rightful response. When we humbly place ourselves at God's mercy, we answer as God desires. Our God will then forgive us according to His "unfailing love."

Share your experience now at
HungerNoMoreBook.com.

MAY 9

*"Wash away all my iniquity
and cleanse me from my sin."*
—Psalm 51:2

We cannot forgive our own sins. We're just not that powerful. As limited human beings, we slip in ways that require outside assistance. Many have turned to counselors, priests, or other solutions for forgiveness, but there is only One whose answer is adequate. David knew his forgiveness did not depend on a human solution; it depended on God.

In David's words, "Wash away all my iniquity and cleanse me from my sin." This is our model still today. We dare not make excuses for our sins. We must be cleansed from them. God longs for us to turn to Him as the solution to our sin problem. When we do, the blood of Jesus can cleanse us from all unrighteousness. He will cleanse us from our sin.

Share your experience now at
HungerNoMoreBook.com.

"For I know my transgressions,
and my sin is always before me."
—Psalm 51:3

Today's political leaders have become masters of apologizing without apologizing. Carefully crafted press statements address the most heinous of issues without specifically mentioning a person's wrongdoing or accepting blame for harm done. To a different degree, many of us do the same with our problems, glossing over them with smooth words and facing them with hardened hearts.

Yet David acknowledged his sin. Rather than tiptoeing around the issue, he assumed full responsibility for the wrongs he had done. Once he had accepted responsibility for his sin, he could sincerely seek God's forgiveness. Is there an area in which we are failing to acknowledge our personal sins? If so, let us accept responsibility today, turning to God's forgiveness as our solution and redemption.

Share your experience now at
HungerNoMoreBook.com.

"Against you, you only, have I sinned."
—Psalm 51:4

All of our sins are ultimately against God. While our wrongs often hurt other people, every wrong committed dishonors God. This is why David could say, "Against you, you only, have I sinned." His sin was not just an issue between David and other people; it was a personal issue between him and God.

When we see our sin as wrongdoing against God, we are compelled to take sin more seriously. Our wrongs are against the One who sent Jesus to die for our wrongs. Our earthly flaws are against our heavenly Father. Let us not take sin lightly. Let us pursue what is right, holy, and true. Let us seek to honor our God, the One who redeems us from all sin.

Share your experience now at
HungerNoMoreBook.com.

"Cleanse me with hyssop, and I will be clean;
wash me, and I will be whiter than snow."
—Psalm 51:7

Sin makes us feel dirty. It creates an ugly layer of filth that covers our soul and separates us from full devotion to our Lord. This is why David wrote, "Cleanse me with hyssop and I will be clean; wash me, and I will be whiter than snow." Hyssop was applied in a cleaning process that removed dirt from the body. God's washing would make David as white as snow, perhaps the purest white he could envision in his culture.

If the Lord washes us, we are completely and totally clean. He does not cleanse partially, leaving a gray residue. He does not cleanse some today and then some tomorrow. God makes us clean. Let us look to Him as the One who redeems us and offers new life.

Share your experience now at
HungerNoMoreBook.com.

"Create in me a pure heart, O God,
and renew a steadfast spirit within me."
—Psalm 51:10

Only God can make our hearts pure. We were born with a sin nature and have stumbled throughout our lives. Apart from the Lord, we would stand hopeless against sin and its impact. Yet God can create a pure heart within us. He can renew our spirit: "Create in me a pure heart, O God, and renew a right spirit within me."

A steadfast spirit is one that is steady and stable. Unlike a baby taking its first steps alone with much wobbling, we find God's hand guiding us along a path that keeps us close to Him. Let us walk closely with Him today, hand in hand with the One who cleanses us and creates in us a pure heart.

Share your experience now at
HungerNoMoreBook.com.

"Restore to me the joy of your salvation."
—Psalm 51:12

Do you remember when you first came to faith in Jesus? What was it like? How did it feel? You likely had a new sense of joy at the removal of guilt in your life and in discovering the purpose God has for you. It is a wonderful, uplifting season of fresh faith.

Many of us find that this initial emotion fades over time. We still have faith, yet we lack the feelings we once had. David acknowledged this: "Restore to me the joy of your salvation." Let this be our prayer today as well. What if everyone who read these words took the time to remember the joy salvation brings? Let it begin today in your life. Let this joy live today in you.

Share your experience now at
HungerNoMoreBook.com.

May 15

*"I will teach transgressors your ways,
so that sinners will turn back to you."*
—Psalm 51:13

To experience revival, we must lift up God among those who do not live for Him. David declared, "I will teach transgressors your ways, so that sinners will turn back to you." To reach others, David knew it was vital to teach God's truth.

The same is true at the personal level. If we wish to live with a renewed heart, we must grow in God's ways from God's Word. Learning from Scripture is listening to the inspired words of God. In them, we learn more of who He is and how He desires for us to live. Let us commit our lives to a renewed walk with God. Let it include a deep hunger for His Word.

Share your experience now at
HungerNoMoreBook.com.

May 16

"Open my lips, Lord, and my mouth
will declare your praise."
—Psalm 51:15

Have you ever thought about the idea that we even need God's help for us to praise Him? We would never worship Him unless God first placed the desire in our hearts to do so. As David wrote, "Open my lips, Lord, and my mouth will declare your praise."

If you are struggling to focus on God, ask Him to give you focus. Ask Him for a desire to desire Him. Often it is in acknowledging our need for passion that we begin to renew passion. When we seek to seek Him, we show we are on the path toward praise, a path that leads to a deeper experience in the presence of our Lord. Ask Him to open your lips and center your heart upon Him.

Share your experience now at
HungerNoMoreBook.com.

"You do not delight in sacrifice, or I would bring it."
—Psalm 51:16

The Jewish faith was built around a system of ritual sacrifices. There was an animal or grain sacrifice for every offense against God. Over time, many people began to use these physical offerings as a substitute for a heart devoted to the Lord. David knew this: "You do not delight in sacrifice, or I would bring it."

David acknowledged that it was the attitude of his heart that mattered more than the offering he gave in a ritual. The same remains true today. Our good deeds or donations cannot compete with a heart devoted to God. There is no alternative other than a life of integrity before Him. Let us not attempt to substitute deeds for dedicated devotion; let our foremost desire be to honor the Lord.

Share your experience now at
HungerNoMoreBook.com.

"My sacrifice, O God, is a broken spirit."
—Psalm 51:17

Rather than offering an animal to acknowledge his sins, David offered his life: "My sacrifice, O God, is a broken spirit." He knew the more difficult task was a devoted life, not a devoted offering. David's offer was to give the energy of his life to serve God. This attitude would later be known as part of what made him a person in tune with God's own heart.

David was not perfect, but he was passionate. Likewise, we are called to serve as imperfect, passionate followers of our Lord. We will often fail, but our heart should be clear to all—we are giving our all to God. Let us live with a heart that beats to the rhythm of our Lord.

Share your experience now at
HungerNoMoreBook.com.

MAY 19

*"A broken and contrite heart you,
God, will not despise."*
—Psalm 51:17

What attitude does God expect of us? Humility and brokenness are His desire. David wrote, "A broken and contrite heart you, God, will not despise." The path to being lifted up and made whole requires us to bow ourselves before Him. His desire is that we make Him our top desire.

It was in serving his own selfish ends that David found himself in need of God's forgiveness. Yet even then God extended grace when David's heart was broken. Let us follow David's example as we address our Father in prayer. When we come before our Lord in humility, we need not fear rejection. He will not despise us. As with David, God's healing will begin the moment we offer God our brokenness.

Share your experience now at
HungerNoMoreBook.com.

"You will delight in the sacrifices of the righteous."
—Psalm 51:19

Only those who bow before God in humility can walk before Him in confidence. It was only after David confessed his sins before the Lord that we read, "You will delight in the sacrifices of the righteous." Confession of sin precedes confidence before the Savior.

When we seek to worship God without a clean heart, our words stand as inauthentic. Dare we sing "I Surrender All" or "Here I Am to Worship" and not truly surrender and offer our genuine worship to our Lord? He knows our hearts. We have no need to hide or perform for His pleasure. He delights in the sacrifices of the righteous. Our goal must be to truly seek Him, to live with righteousness, as we worship Him today.

Share your experience now at
HungerNoMoreBook.com.

May 21

"The righteous will see and fear."
—Psalm 52:6

When those who do evil are brought to justice, "The righteous will see and fear." David wrote Psalm 52 following Doeg's injustice of killing God's priests who aided David and his men. David knew God would bring judgment upon Doeg for his action. When it happened, it would elicit fear among God's people.

Often, when an unjust leader's life ends, people rejoice. But here David emphasizes another reaction—fear. This fear causes those who follow God's ways to continue to live for the Lord, knowing that there is a judgment for those who do evil. We are called to both pursue what is right as well as to reject what is evil. A godly fear drives us to deeper love for God.

Share your experience now at
HungerNoMoreBook.com.

"I trust in God's unfailing love for ever and ever."
—Psalm 52:8

Trust is tough. Once trust has been broken by multiple people on multiple occasions, believing in anyone or anything becomes increasingly difficult. Much of the skepticism of our world can be traced back to broken trust.

Yet David calls us to a childlike faith in our Lord: "I trust in God's unfailing love for ever and ever." He trusted in the One who could be completely believed for all eternity. God's love is unfailing and His kingdom will never end. Unlike human relationships that inevitably let us down, the Lord offers a perfect relationship deserving of our total trust and allegiance. Let us renew our trust in His unfailing love. He will never let us down in this life or the next.

Share your experience now at
HungerNoMoreBook.com.

*"For what you have done I will always praise you
in the presence of your faithful people."*
—Psalm 52:9

Even if God never did another good thing in our lives, we could spend the rest of this life praising Him for what He has already done. Because of this, David could pen, "For what you have done I will always praise you." He was confident there would never be a point at which he would run out of reasons to celebrate the Lord's greatness.

Interestingly, David also adds that this praise would be "in the presence of your faithful people." Only those who love the Lord would rejoice at David's praises. We, too, rejoice together with our spiritual family as we celebrate the great works of our Lord. Let us encourage one another today with the Lord's praises. May we never cease to worship Him.

Share your experience now at
HungerNoMoreBook.com.

"I will hope in your name, for your name is good."
—Psalm 52:9

Not only is God good; even His name is reason to rejoice: "I will hope in your name, for your name is good." Many names are used of the Lord throughout Scripture. Common titles in the Psalms include the Lord, God, God Most High, Shepherd, and King. Each name highlights a unique attribute of our heavenly Father in ways that lead to further praise.

Names tell us much about a person. An individual's last name reveals family connections. A first or middle name may shine insight on names important to a parent. A nickname often leads to an insightful story. But God's names teach us about the One who created and loves us. Let us hope in His name, for His name is good.

Share your experience now at
HungerNoMoreBook.com.

"The fool says in his heart, 'There is no God.'"
—Psalm 53:1

David tells us that denying God's existence is not only inaccurate, it is foolish: "The fool says in his heart, 'There is no God.'" Only God explains the existence of our universe, our planet, and our lives. Only God can account for the beauty of the mountains and seas.

The atheist is not a person who trusts in mere intellectual reasoning; the atheist assumes knowledge of the entire known universe. In their view, there is no God and he or she knows there is no God for reasons developed by human intellect. Yet our minds cannot even comprehend the complexities of the human mind, much less the universe. God exists. Atheism is not a matter of the mind; it is a matter of the heart.

Share your experience now at
HungerNoMoreBook.com.

*"Everyone has turned away, all have become corrupt;
there is no one who does good, not even one."*

—Psalm 53:3

God's Word is clear: without Him, we would never seek Him: "There is no one who does good, not even one." Our salvation is completely dependent upon the Lord. He must first place a desire within us to seek Him. He then continues to sustain us when we do come to faith in Christ and follow Him. He not only gives salvation; He is our salvation.

When we first come to faith in Christ, we often think it was simply of our own choosing. Only later do we realize we would have never taken that step of faith apart from His grace drawing us near to Him. Let us thank Him for His salvation today and share His love with those in our lives who have yet to seek Him.

Share your experience now at
HungerNoMoreBook.com.

MAY 27

"Surely God is my help;
the Lord is the one who sustains me."
—Psalm 54:4

When life gets us down, how do we keep going? God. The same Creator who designed us from our mother's womb is the One who sustains us each moment of each day. Our heart both begins to beat and continues to beat at His command. We need not fear whether we have the strength to endure; it is His strength that keeps us standing when we are about to fall.

Further, His sustaining includes His help: "Surely God is my help; the Lord is the one who sustains me." His sustaining power and help parallel one another in our lives. He helps us by sustaining us and sustains us by helping us. Let us move forward trusting in His power for our day.

Share your experience now at
HungerNoMoreBook.com.

"Listen to my prayer, O God, do not ignore my plea."
—Psalm 55:1

Though God always hears our prayers, we sometimes feel the need to remind God to listen. Whether the answer has been long to come or the situation is desperate, we can all relate to David's plea: "Listen to my prayer, O God, do not ignore my plea." David knew God intimately, yet even he struggled with whether the Lord was listening to his needs.

As David repeatedly discovered throughout his spiritual sojourn, God listened and did not ignore his requests. Answers arrived in the Lord's perfect timing to provide for David's every need. What David experienced can encourage us today. We may feel the need to remind God to hear us, but we can also rest assured His answer is already on the way.

Share your experience now at
HungerNoMoreBook.com.

"My heart is in anguish within me."
—Psalm 55:4

Heart trouble is often the worst kind of trouble. A physical wound will heal over time, but the wounds of the heart can linger for years. Scars can form; infection can fester. David expressed, "My heart is in anguish within me." In these situations, only the Divine Surgeon can intervene and make the necessary repairs.

God would heal the ache of his soul, but David's emotions would later return with a new situation for the Lord to address. We may find ourselves in a similar scenario. Crying out to God, we experience the response of His holy, perfect love. Yet we continue to return with each day's hurts. Let us take courage that today's anguish is in God's hands. There is no problem He cannot heal.

Share your experience now at
HungerNoMoreBook.com.

"As for me, I call to God, and the LORD saves me."
—Psalm 55:16

Our calls to God are never left unanswered, placed on hold, or redirected to an automated response system. Rather than ignoring our needs, He invites us to communicate with Him. David's relationship with the Lord expressed both sorrow and joy: "As for me, I call to God, and the LORD saves me." Never left alone, David could count on the Lord to answer.

Why do we often assume the worst when we pray? We ask for help, then wonder if God hears us. If He does, maybe He doesn't care or will deny our request to intervene. But our Father's love is perfect, as is His hearing. He listens to our cries. When He does, we can count on Him to save.

Share your experience now at
HungerNoMoreBook.com.

May 31

"He rescues me unharmed from
the battle waged against me."
—Psalm 55:18

Battles take a toll. Just ask any soldier. Veterans struggle with both the physical and emotional scars for a lifetime. This makes David's statement much more significant when we realize what he is communicating. He wrote, "He rescues me unharmed from the battle waged against me." God not only allowed David to survive; He rescued him unharmed.

God allows us to endure pain in ways we often cannot understand. Yet He also rescues us on many occasions in ways we cannot understand. The crisis should have been much worse, yet it was not. The crash should have ended our lives, yet we walked away. God's grace surprises us at times. Let us look out for a fresh surprise from Him today.

Share your experience now at
HungerNoMoreBook.com.

*"Cast your cares on the LORD
and he will sustain you."*
—Psalm 55:22

God not only cares about us; He encourages us to cast our cares on Him: "Cast your cares on the LORD and he will sustain you." Our Father carries our concerns and us. He is perfectly empowered to handle both.

When life's struggles pull us down, the Lord serves not as our ladder, but as our leader. He picks us up, moves us to safety, and places our feet on solid ground. We do not need to climb out of our pit; we only need to reach up. He will lift us up. He will sustain us. Today, let us not carry the burdens that weigh us down. We dare not lift them on our own. Let us cast our cares on the Lord.

Share your experience now at
HungerNoMoreBook.com.

JUNE 2

"When I am afraid, I put my trust in you."
—Psalm 56:3

Fear is the result of uncertainty. We don't know if it's safe to drive during a storm, so we fear the condition of the roads. We're unsure if there is enough money to pay a medical bill, so we fear what will happen. These types of fears continue until the uncertainty is resolved.

Yet David notes how he dealt with the fear of being seized by his enemies: "When I am afraid, I put my trust in you." He knew God's certainty could handle his life's uncertainty. No matter the magnitude of the fear, the Lord stood as a solid foundation upon which David could place his fears. When fears enters our lives today, let us respond like David. Let us trust in the Lord.

Share your experience now at
HungerNoMoreBook.com.

JUNE 3

"In God I trust and am not afraid.
What can man do to me?"
—Psalm 56:11

The Philistines were known as formidable opponents in battle. Their violent ways had led to graphic stories of horrific treatment toward enemies and prisoners of war. David knew these foes well, yet refused to tremble: "in God I trust and am not afraid. What can man do to me?"

We often see a difficult challenge and choose fear. David saw his challenge as nothing compared to God's power. The same God who empowered him to defeat the Philistine giant Goliath could save him once again. Our foes may overwhelm us, yet they are small in comparison to God's power. When we face impossible odds, let us not look at the size of our problem; let us look at the size of our God.

Share your experience now at
HungerNoMoreBook.com.

JUNE 4

"For you have delivered me from death
and my feet from stumbling,
that I may walk before God in the light of life."
—Psalm 56:13

God does not rescue us so we can continue to sin; He delivers us so we can extend His salvation. When David faced death, God redeemed him from the hands of his enemies. Why? "For you have delivered me from death and my feet from stumbling, that I may walk before God in the light of life." The One delivered David from death and stumbling to walk according to His plans.

David was saved so he could serve. We are as well. Let us not live to meet our own desires, but to fulfill the desires of our heavenly Father. His plan of redemption includes His plan for our vocation. Let us "walk before God."

Share your experience now at
HungerNoMoreBook.com.

"I will take refuge in the shadow of your wings."
—Psalm 57:1

Safety comes in our nearness to God, not in our distance from our enemies. Security lies in the wings of God, not the walls of a fortress. David's plan was not to flee from his earthly foe, but to run to his heavenly Father: "I will take refuge in the shadow of your wings."

Just as a young bird clings next to the safety of its mother's wings, so we are called to nestle near the side of our Lord. When we do, we find protection from life's enemies and elements. In Him, we find our refuge, our rest, and our redemption. Let us not seek to fly in our own strength; let us cling in the shadow of God's wings. He is our refuge.

Share your experience now at
HungerNoMoreBook.com.

JUNE 6

"I will praise you, Lord, among the nations;
I will sing of you among the peoples."
—Psalm 57:9

Today's top headlines spread across the world regardless of national boundaries. When a war begins on one side of the planet, reports instantly reach citizens multiple time zones away. When an earthquake devastates a nation, untouched nations quickly hear reports of the disaster.

When the Lord spared David from disaster, his response was similar in desire: "I will praise you, Lord, among the nations; I will sing of you among the nations." David wanted the people of every tribe and territory to know of the greatness of his God. When the Lord touches our hearts, we are compelled to do the same. Our desire, like David's, is to tell everyone who will listen of what God has done in our lives.

Share your experience now at
HungerNoMoreBook.com.

JUNE 7

"The righteous will be glad when they are avenged."
—Psalm 58:10

When the wicked face vengeance, there is a sense in which God's people experience joy. This is not due to the pain endured by the wicked, but because it shows that doing what is right has an advantage over doing what is evil. As David wrote, "The righteous will be glad when they are avenged."

The struggle to live God's way makes it tempting to choose a lesser path. Yet when those who have chosen to do wrong experience judgment, it strengthens our resolve to keep our feet firmly planted in the direction of God's will. Let us not grow weary in doing good this day. Let us look forward toward our Lord. Let us experience our joy in doing His will.

Share your experience now at
HungerNoMoreBook.com.

JUNE 8

"Surely the righteous still are rewarded."
—Psalm 58:11

There is an old quote that states, "Righteousness is its own reward." While this may be true, David also taught, "Surely the righteous still are rewarded." Those who live God's way will experience God's reward at the proper time.

Contrary to our world's teachings, however, these rewards do not always appear in this life. The Lord has not promised us earthly riches or perfect health. Instead, we are guaranteed eternity in God's presence when we believe in His Son Jesus, along with heavenly rewards beyond our comprehension for faithfulness. When the wicked seem to prosper, let us remember that "the righteous still are rewarded." Doing God's will brings riches that exceed any earthly wealth. Living for the Lord leads to treasures that transcend this world.

Share your experience now at
HungerNoMoreBook.com.

June 9

"Be my fortress against those who are attacking me."
—Psalm 59:1

The ancient fortress was the greatest place of security against an attacking army. This explains why David wrote, "Be my fortress against those who are attacking me." During his times of battle, God was his source of strength, his defense against those who would harm him.

Too often, we attempt to tackle our problems in our own power apart from God's protection. When we fail, we wonder why God didn't protect us. The problem? Our own failure to turn to Him as our fortress. We don't fight and then ask God to help. We run to God before the fight begins. Let us count on our Lord for our help today. Let Him serve as our fortress in today's attacks.

Share your experience now at
HungerNoMoreBook.com.

JUNE 10

"My God on whom I can rely."
—Psalm 59:17

We rely on people we trust. We choose mechanics because of their ability to get the job done right. We select doctors based on their ability to diagnose our health needs. Likewise, we not only trust God initially; we rely on Him. David called the Lord "my God on whom I can rely."

Despite David's many physical battles and political turmoil, he knew he could turn to the Lord as a reliable helper during times of need. God was always faithful, always right, always perfect. When we face difficult situations, we may find it tempting to rely on our own power. Let us not forget that it is God who we rely upon, not ourselves. He is our Rock, our God on whom we rely.

Share your experience now at
HungerNoMoreBook.com.

*"Save us and help us with your right hand,
that those you love may be delivered."*
—Psalm 60:5

God saves us because He loves us. It has nothing to do with our goodness or nobility, our achievements or agility. Our salvation depends completely upon our Savior. David writes, "Save us and help us with your right hand, that those you love may be delivered." He did not appeal to his own good works; David appealed to the Lord's love.

When we cry out to our heavenly Father, let us not seek to convince Him to respond because of our efforts to please Him. Our deeds will not cause God to love us more; our sins will not cause God to love us less. Rather, we appeal to His love. The same love that saved us is the save love that rescues us.

Share your experience now at
HungerNoMoreBook.com.

JUNE 12

"With God we will gain the victory."
—Psalm 60:12

Victory is determined by God. Whether the odds are in our favor or against us, it is not our strength but the Lord's that decides the outcome. As David wrote, "With God we will gain the victory." He knew his success depended completely upon the Lord's intervention, not his human ingenuity. Without the Lord, no plan would be adequate.

We falter when we forget our success is in God's hands rather than our own. We work hard, follow the right steps, then fall short of our goal. This is often because the goal was of our own making, not God's. Let us not count on our own plans for success today; let us look to our Savior. Only with God can we count on victory.

Share your experience now at
HungerNoMoreBook.com.

June 13

*"From the ends of the earth I call to you,
I call as my heart grows faint."*
—Psalm 61:2

David did not only look to God when it was convenient; he sought the Lord at every moment. Regardless of location or situation, David's passion for the Lord God remained the same: "From the ends of the earth I call to you, I call as my heart grows faint."

The "ends of the earth" was a phrase commonly used to indicate "all over the earth." No matter where David journeyed, his God was the focus. "As my heart grows faint" referred to his emotional condition—a time of personal struggle. In his weakness, the Lord served as his strength. Wherever our steps take us today, let us know God is there. In our fragile moments, He is eager to listen and reply.

Share your experience now at
HungerNoMoreBook.com.

"I long to dwell in your tent forever."
—Psalm 61:4

In the ancient Middle East, people commonly lived in tents rather than homes. Such housing both allowed for mobility and was easier to build than a house of brick or stone. Even as king, David sought God's presence over his national headquarters: "I long to dwell in your tent forever."

His request includes three essential aspects. First, David longed. This was not a wish, but a passion. Second, he desired to dwell with God. Where the Lord lived is where David wanted to live. Third, David longed to live with God forever. His focus was not on wealth or worldly success, but on his future with his heavenly Father. Today, let us not live content with this world's possessions; let us long for our eternal home.

Share your experience now at
HungerNoMoreBook.com.

*"Yes, my soul, find rest in God;
my hope comes from him."*
—Psalm 62:5

Rest is found in God. When we are spiritually restless, only He satisfies. When we are exhausted, only He energizes: "Yes, my soul, find rest in God; my hope comes from him." David certainly found many occasions in which he required physical and emotional strength to continue. He did not rely alone on a physical resource to increase his stamina; he counted on God.

Too often, we find ourselves exhausted, longing for relief. Entire industries are built around keeping people awake when needed. Others are designed to help people sleep when they can't. Though such help can at times be beneficial, they do not replace our need to find our rest in God. Our hope cannot be found in what this world offers; our hope comes from Him.

Share your experience now at
HungerNoMoreBook.com.

*"I thirst for you, my whole being longs for you,
in a dry and parched land where there is no water."*
—Psalm 63:1

David thirsted for God. Though he knew the Lord, he regularly craved a deeper connection with him. In his words, "I thirst for you, my whole being longs for you." He compared his desire to the thirst of a person in "a dry and parched land where there is no water."

From his myriad of outdoor experiences, David may have been intimately acquainted with such thirst. Whether in his youth as a shepherd or on the run from Saul and his army, David often lived under extreme conditions that would have influenced him to express these words. Without water, we cannot live. Likewise, apart from God, we cannot survive or thrive. Let us thirst for God today. He is the only one who can satisfy.

Share your experience now at
HungerNoMoreBook.com.

JUNE 17

*"All people will fear; they will proclaim the works
of God and ponder what he has done."*
—Psalm 64:9

There is a proper place for fear in our relationship with God. This is the fear that David mentioned when he wrote, "All people will fear; they will proclaim the works of God and ponder what he has done." An appropriate fear of the Lord leads to telling others about Him and reflecting on His greatness. It is a fear that leads to a closer walk with God, not running away from God.

A healthy fear of the Lord causes us to treat Him with proper respect. He is much more than a friend or moral influence; He is our Father and Master. We dare not live in a way that dishonors the One who made us. Let us live in proper fear of the Lord.

Share your experience now at
HungerNoMoreBook.com.

JUNE 18

"When we were overwhelmed by sins,
you forgave our transgressions."
—Psalm 65:3

Sin separates us from God. Apart from His forgiveness, we cannot experience His fellowship. As David explained, "When we were overwhelmed by sins, you forgave our transgressions." God's forgiveness is the difference between sin conquering us and us conquering sin.

This tremendous truth stands at the core of our relationship with God because sin can overwhelm. The guilt of past failures can consume our thoughts and our actions, even years later. Yet this does not have to be the case. When God forgives, He removes our guilt. He cleanses our stains. Instead, we experience the joy of new life. Let us live in this newness of life today. Let us proclaim the greatness of being forgiven of our sins.

Share your experience now at
HungerNoMoreBook.com.

"Sing the glory of his name; make his praise glorious."
—Psalm 66:2

Many of the Psalms focus on God's glory. Why? Glory is God's distinction, His renown. He is unique in the entire universe as the One who is glorious, and stands worthy for His creation to glorify Him. As the psalmist wrote, "Sing the glory of his name; make his praise glorious."

When we give glory to God, we mean that we give praise to Him. We honor Him not only for what He has done, but also for who He is. He is without fault and without beginning or end. He is our Creator, Redeemer, Shepherd, and Healer. He is worthy of praise by all for He has created all. Let us communicate our praise to Him—and to others—this day. Let us make His praise glorious.

Share your experience now at
HungerNoMoreBook.com.

JUNE 20

*"Praise be to God, who has not rejected my prayer
or withheld his love from me!"*
—Psalm 66:20

There are many reasons to praise God. In Psalm 66, two distinct details highlighted by the writer include God hearing his prayer and God's love: "Praise be to God, who has not rejected my prayer or withheld his love from me!" While others had rejected David or shown hatred toward Him, the Lord had received Him with the perfect compassion of a caring Father.

When Samuel arrived at the home of David's father, Jesse, to anoint one of his sons as king, David was not initially even considered. On another occasion, David's brothers mocked him when he delivered supplies during battle. Yet God accepted him, just as He accepts us. No matter our past hurts, our Lord can heal. He will not withhold His love from us.

Share your experience now at
HungerNoMoreBook.com.

*"May God be gracious to us and bless us
and make his face shine on us."*
—Psalm 67:1

One prayer universal to all people is the request for a blessing. We all desire God's hand of success upon our lives and our efforts. As the psalmist wrote, "May God be gracious to us and bless us and make his face shine upon us."

In this request, we find three distinct and important requests. First, the psalmist asks for God's grace. Second, he asks for God's blessing. Third, he asks for God's face to shine upon us, a request for the Lord's favor. God's face shining upon us includes the idea of looking upon us in joy. We need all three. Let us ask for God's grace, blessing, and favor. Let us also seek to shine His grace, blessing, and favor on others.

Share your experience now at
HungerNoMoreBook.com.

JUNE 22

"May the righteous be glad and rejoice before God;
may they be happy and joyful."
—Psalm 68:3

Those who know God should be known for their joy. Following God can be difficult, but it should not be depressing. Despite our moments of suffering and struggle, we are compelled to serve our heavenly Father with intense joy. The psalmist declared, "May the righteous be glad and rejoice before God; may they be happy and joyful."

When we walk with the Lord, we find a resilience that carries us through life's difficulties. Our God is with us in our pain and allows us to participate in His joy despite our pain. Even the worst of life's tragedies can be endured by those who know the Lord. Why? Because in the midst of hurt, we also have hope. God is our strength and our joy.

Share your experience now at
HungerNoMoreBook.com.

*"A father to the fatherless, a defender of widows,
is God in his holy dwelling."*
—Psalm 68:5

Orphans and widows are of special concern to God throughout Scripture. He looks at those without family as a special part of His spiritual family. Even in His holy dwelling, God is concerned for those in the most vulnerable of situations: "A father to the fatherless, a defender of widows, is God in his holy dwelling."

If God showers special concern on those in vulnerable situations, should we not share the same compassion? Those who follow God must care about His cares. Whether the fatherless, a widow, or another person in distress, who is it God would have us to help today? Let us make His top priorities our top priorities. Let we who love God show His love to those in need.

Share your experience now at
HungerNoMoreBook.com.

JUNE 24

"Praise be to the Lord, to God our Savior,
who daily bears our burdens."
—Psalm 68:19

In ancient times, both camels and donkeys were animals used to carry the loads of travelers over long distances. A person could carry only a tiny amount of luggage in comparison to one of these creatures. A camel or donkey could share the load and carry the burden much better.

David expressed this principle in spiritual terms: "Praise be to the Lord, to the God our Savior, who daily bears our burdens." The fact that God could daily carry the problems of his life caused Him to sing out in praise. Let us do the same. May we give our burdens to the Lord, for He can easily carry our load. May we rejoice that He does, giving praise to God our Savior.

Share your experience now at
HungerNoMoreBook.com.

JUNE 25

*"The God of Israel gives
power and strength to his people."*
—Psalm 68:35

The greatest strength is not found on earth, but in heaven. Power does not originate with us, but with God. This is why David could share, "The God of Israel gives power and strength to his people." The nation of Israel had been the result of God's ability to lead them from slavery to statehood.

Further, David would have personally known the result of God's power in his life. From tending sheep to defeating Goliath to his battles to becoming king, David knew that the Lord served as the One who gave the victory. In each situation, the odds were stacked against David. Yet he continued to succeed. Why? The strength of the Lord. When we feel weak, let us remember—He is our source of strength.

Share your experience now at
HungerNoMoreBook.com.

*"Save me, O God, for the waters
have come up to my neck."*
—Psalm 69:1

In David's time, most kids didn't grow up learning to swim. In fact, he may have never been a swimmer himself. The idea of deep water may have frightened him since he wrote, "Save me, O God, for the waters have come up to my neck." Like a child tiptoeing too far into the deep end of a pool and crying for help, David expressed a situation in which he was in too much danger to rescue himself.

Do you feel overwhelmed at the situation you currently face? Is the water too deep for you to escape on your own? God is the answer. He is our Lifeguard. Like a loving parent rescuing their child from dangerous waters, God will save in our time of need.

Share your experience now at
HungerNoMoreBook.com.

JUNE 27

"Rescue me from the mire, do not let me sink."
—Psalm 69:14

Rescue evokes images of an exciting scene. A person pulled from a burning building or a lost climber retrieved from the mountains makes for a great story. However, in every case the rescue involved a painful situation for the one in need of help. There was no excitement at the time it happened—only fear.

When David wrote, "Rescue me from the mire, do not let me sink," he did not have in mind an exciting experience. He envisioned a frightening encounter. Apart from God's intervention, the situation was hopeless. Without His help, there would be no escape. Do you feel like you are sinking? Are you in need of rescue? As David did, let us call out to God. The Lord is our Rescuer.

Share your experience now at
HungerNoMoreBook.com.

JUNE 28

*"The LORD hears the needy
and does not despise his captive people."*
—Psalm 69:33

Those who live in need are often neglected by others. They are ignored on the streets or on the bus. People fear they will ask for money or pose a threat. While there are many noble exceptions, those in need are historically overlooked by the vast majority of society.

But what is true of society is not true of our Savior: "The LORD hears the needy and does not despise his captive people." God listens to the plight of the poor and the slave. He pays special attention to their situation. Our Father wants to meet our needs. He also wants us to reach out to meet the needs of others. May we seek to do both in our lives today.

Share your experience now at
HungerNoMoreBook.com.

"You are my help and my deliverer;
LORD, do not delay."
—Psalm 70:5

Do you ever feel like God is running late? You're not alone. David once wrote, "You are my help and my deliverer; LORD, do not delay." From David's perspective, it felt like God was falling behind. He felt the pressure of the moment. God needed to answer now.

God always hears our pleas, but He doesn't always show up when we please. Sometimes our slow is His fast. What we think would be perfect timing is not yet His time. He has not forgotten us and will never fail us. He will help. He will deliver. Our God will not delay. Let us not doubt His response; let us continue to pray to Him until He responds. He is listening in our time of need.

Share your experience now at
HungerNoMoreBook.com.

"Be my rock of refuge, to which I can always go."
—Psalm 71:3

Is there ever a time we cannot turn to God? Not according to psalmist. "Be my rock of refuge, to which I can always go." David lived with the confidence that God's office is never closed; His phone lines are never busy; His lines of communication are never down. God is there before, during, and after the crisis.

In addition to always being available, God always shows Himself strong. As a rock of refuge, He is the unbreakable One we can turn to when everything else breaks down. His fortress cannot be defeated, His powers can never be thwarted. When we are weak, He is strong. Let us turn to Him in our weakness today. We can always look to Him.

Share your experience now at
HungerNoMoreBook.com.

"Your righteousness, God, reaches to the heavens, you who have done great things. Who is like you, God?"
—Psalm 71:19

God is great and what He does is great. He not only performs righteousness; He is righteous. The psalmist declared, "Your righteousness, God, reaches to the heavens, you have done great things." We do not question His character, only His competition: "Who is like you, God?"

When we truly grasp God's greatness in comparison to all of life's problems, we can live with a deep sense of confidence even in the midst of tragedy. Sickness strikes, yet God can heal. Conflict can inflict pain, yet our Lord can bring peace. Even death can only end this life; it cannot remove us from God's hand. Our view of God determines our view of life. Let us live with eyes wide open today.

Share your experience now at
HungerNoMoreBook.com.

*"He will rescue them from oppression and violence,
for precious is their blood in his sight."*
—Psalm 72:14

God cares about our soul and our body. At times, we treat one as more important than the other, as if God desires our prayers yet is unconcerned with whether we eat, sleep, or function in ways that honor Him with our body. Yet our Father cares for our entirety. "He will rescue them from oppression and violence, for precious is their blood in his sight."

These words center on rescue from harm, yet also connect with God's longing for our physical well-being. When we endure sleepless nights, He desires to give us rest. When our health falters from a difficult day of work, He seeks healing for our exhausted muscles. Every fiber of our being is of infinite value to God.

Share your experience now at
HungerNoMoreBook.com.

"Praise be to the Lord God, the God of Israel,
who alone does marvelous deeds."
—Psalm 72:18

One of the primary ways we praise God is for what He has done in our lives. This means that in order to increase the depth of our praise, we must increase our awareness of how He is working in us. As the psalmist echoed, "Praise be to the Lord God, the God of Israel, who alone does marvelous deeds."

A simple method to reflect on God's work in our lives is to write down a list. Create a list of 10 or 20 or 50 works the Lord has done for you recently. As you do, you'll discover your heart overflowing with thanksgiving. He has done the work; we need only do the work of praising Him. He has certainly blessed us with many marvelous deeds.

Share your experience now at
HungerNoMoreBook.com.

JULY 4

"Surely God is good to Israel,
to those who are pure in heart."
—Psalm 73:1

Sometimes we need a gentle reminder that God's blessing is upon those whose heart is pure. When those who neglect or mock the Lord appear to prosper, there is a temptation to join in their ways. When trials arise in our walk with the Lord, the easy way out very much feels like the easy way out.

Yet the psalmist Asaph wrote, "Surely God is good to Israel, to those who are pure in heart." Upon reflection on the lives of both the just and the unjust, he was reminded that those who follow the Lord are those whose ways are truly blessed. No other substitute satisfies. God's goodness transcends the temporary pleasures of evil. Let us seek to live as those "pure in heart."

Share your experience now at
HungerNoMoreBook.com.

JULY 5

"I am always with you;
you hold me by my right hand."
—Psalm 73:23

It is an overwhelming reality to realize God is always with us. There is not one moment He steps away or vanishes from sight. As Asaph wrote, "I am always with you; you hold me by my right hand." God is there, He is near, He is our constant companion.

So why do we not always feel close to God? Part of the problem is the frailty of our human emotions. Often weak and unreliable, our thoughts tell us God has left even though He holds our hand. Other times, we allow circumstances to bring doubt into our hearts, questioning how God could allow trouble while being with us. Yet He has never left. Let us continue to follow the lead of His loving hand.

Share your experience now at
HungerNoMoreBook.com.

"Whom have I in heaven but you?
And earth has nothing I desire besides you."
—Psalm 73:25

Our ultimate desire is for God. As our Creator, our souls long for connection with Him. As our Sustainer, our spirits seek connection with its source of strength. As our Redeemer, our hearts look to Him with thankfulness. In the psalmist's words, "Whom have I in heaven but you? And earth has nothing I desire besides you."

Nothing in this world or the skies above can compare with the greatness of God's love. Many have sought to follow gods of their own making, whether among the stars in the heavens or created idols of silver or gold. History reveals these creations are nothing more than a substitute for our heart's true longing—the Lord. Let our God serve as our greatest passion.

Share your experience now at
HungerNoMoreBook.com.

"As for me, it is good to be near God."
—Psalm 73:28

Those who come to faith in the Lord later in life often savor Him the most. Why? They have experienced the pain of living without God. Their new life serves as a stark contrast to their former way of life. They live mindful of the psalmist's thought, "As for me, it is good to be near God."

Yet nearness to God is not only important to later converts, but to us all. Though our Lord is ever-present, our degree of passion varies. The daily grind of life seeks to divert our gaze toward other pursuits or problems. However, our greatest problem is often not the problem in front of us. Let us stay focused on Him. It is good to be near God.

Share your experience now at
HungerNoMoreBook.com.

*"But God is my King from long ago;
he brings salvation on the earth."*
—Psalm 74:12

The Psalms offer two recurring themes regarding the nature of our Lord. He is often called King and frequently mentioned as our salvation. These two concepts find their fulfillment in the Lord Jesus, our saving King. The psalmist expressed it this way: "But God is my King from long ago; he brings salvation on the earth."

Little did this psalmist know what would take place years later. The Messiah, Jesus Christ, came to earth as King of the Jews. He offered salvation to the earth. He was despised and rejected, yet proved Himself as Lord by His resurrection. He is King. He does offer salvation. May we live in allegiance to Him and experience the joy of His salvation as we serve Him today.

Share your experience now at
HungerNoMoreBook.com.

"Do not let the oppressed retreat in disgrace;
may the poor and needy praise your name."
—Psalm 74:21

Do you ever feel the need to remind God to look out for you? We all do. Though He knows our every thought, there are times we call out to God to request what we know He has already promised to do. Asaph practiced this when he wrote, "Do not let the oppressed retreat in disgrace; may the poor and needy praise your name."

Asaph was concerned that his nation's enemies would gain victory over God's people. How could God allow those in need to suffer? He knew God cared; He was asking God to act like it. When we see injustice in our lives, we are compelled to respond in a similar matter. May we lift up the needs of the oppressed today.

Share your experience now at
HungerNoMoreBook.com.

July 10

"We praise you, God, we praise you, for your Name is near; people tell of your wonderful deeds."
—Psalm 75:1

Good news does not go unnoticed. When we receive a generous gift from a friend, we spontaneously tell others about it. When a mother gives birth to a child, she cannot help but rejoice and celebrate with family and friends. The same is true regarding the works of God. His mighty acts lead to acts of praise from His people.

The psalmist worded it this way: "We praise you, God, we praise you, for your Name is near; people tell of your wonderful deeds." God is both near and active. He has created us and continues to bless us. Our response is to praise His name, to tell those around us how He is working in our lives.

Share your experience now at
HungerNoMoreBook.com.

"It is you alone who are to be feared."
—Psalm 76:7

With God, we have no one to fear but God. He holds all power; His enemies stand no chance against Him. We have life in full confidence against any foe on earth, yet we bow in reverence to our Father in heaven. As Asaph shared, "It is you alone who are to be feared."

The same Creator who spared Noah's family and the animals in the Flood also brought destruction on all other people. The same God who parted the Red Sea for Moses and the people of Israel also allowed the water to destroy their enemies. God can save us from all enemies, yet this same strength calls us to reverence and fear His name. Let us live in awe before Him this day.

Share your experience now at
HungerNoMoreBook.com.

"When I was in distress, I sought the Lord."
—Psalm 77:2

This life's pains point out our need for God. If our human existence were without struggle, we would find little use for the Lord. Often it is in our greatest points of weakness that we seek the Lord the most. The psalmist expressed, "When I was in distress, I sought the Lord."

Have you ever stopped to consider that God may be using your problems to cause you to seek Him? Would the Creator of the universe allow a particular struggle to create a deeper longing in your life for Him? The same Lord who knows the numbers of hairs on our head seeks to connect with us on a daily basis. Let today's troubles not turn us from God; let them turn us to Him.

Share your experience now at
HungerNoMoreBook.com.

"I will remember the deeds of the LORD;
yes, I will remember your miracles of long ago."
—Psalm 77:11

When life gets us down, recounting the great works of God in our lives can help restore joy. Look back over years past. When did God first become real to you? In what ways has He clearly guided your past to bring you to your present moment? What answers has He given; what unexpected gifts has He provided?

When the psalmist was discouraged, he decided, "I will remember the deeds of the LORD; yes, I will remember your miracles of long ago." His recollection of God's past acts of greatness provided confidence that the Lord would answer once again. If you are waiting for an answer today, look at God's answers in the past. Rest assured He is ready to respond once again.

Share your experience now at
HungerNoMoreBook.com.

JULY 14

"Your ways, God, are holy.
What god is as great as our God?"
—Psalm 77:13

Our modern understanding of the word *holy* fails to reflect the understanding of the ancient Jewish people. To be holy was to be pure, clean from a myriad of regulations that could keep a person from worship in the tabernacle and later the temple. Holiness was the highest and most difficult daily calling of those who lived for the Lord.

This understanding of holiness brings a fresh perspective to the words of the psalmist who declared, "Your ways, God, are holy. What god is as great as our God?" The Lord did not have to seek holiness; He was holy. His ways were holy. No other so-called god compared with Him. Nothing can compete with His greatness. Let us walk in reverent worship of our God.

Share your experience now at
HungerNoMoreBook.com.

*"We will tell the next generation
the praiseworthy deeds of the Lord."*
—Psalm 78:4

There is something significant about the sharing of information from one generation to another. A sacred trust passed down from grandfather to father to child or from grandmother down to granddaughter means much more than content originating from another source.

In Jewish culture, family was responsible to pass down important information within the family. Of greatest regard were the works of the Lord: "We will tell the next generation the praiseworthy deeds of the Lord." What would be the impact of thousands of God's people practicing this tradition today? Let us share the great works of God with those closest to us, that future generations may know and trust in the Lord. Let our goal be to communicate our faith to future generations.

Share your experience now at
HungerNoMoreBook.com.

"So the next generation would know them,
even the children yet to be born,
and they in turn would tell their children."
—Psalm 78:6

Children are a blessing from God. Despite the struggles and obligations of raising a child, the investment is priceless. Grandchildren likewise offer a unique blessing, the opportunity to see the children of our own children, our legacy for the next generation.

Our greatest desire for our children and their children must be that they follow the Lord: "So the next generation would know them, even the children yet to be born, and they in turn would tell their children." Let us live not only to serve God ourselves; let us live to help our children and their children live for God. Through our lives, may their legacy be one that honors the Lord. May those not yet born know our heavenly Father.

Share your experience now at
HungerNoMoreBook.com.

"Then they would put their trust in God and would not forget his deeds but would keep his commands."
—Psalm 78:7

The key to keeping God's commands is not to memorize them, but to put our trust in God. The psalmist wrote, "Then they would put their trust in God and would not forget his deeds but would keep his commands." When we trust the Lord, we follow Him. Our lives are not built upon regulations, but on a relationship.

Perhaps this is why the greatest commandment both in the Law of Moses and also affirmed by Jesus is that we would love the Lord God with all our heart, soul, and strength. It is when we love God that we live for God. As we share His love with others, let us encourage them to place their trust in the Lord.

Share your experience now at
HungerNoMoreBook.com.

*"He guided them with the cloud by day
and with light from the fire all night."*
—Psalm 78:14

The Israelites with Moses lived in the wilderness for 40 years. Every day, God guided them with a cloud during the day and a fire of light at night. Can you imagine? There was no need for a map or GPS. God served as their guide and their light.

In our modern world of technology, we sometimes prefer our tools to the supernatural power God can provide. We would rather find our way with a device rather than with the Lord. Technology can offer wonderful advantages but can also cloud our communications with God. Let us make sure we let nothing block our connection with Him today. Let us seek the God of Israel, the One who guides our path according to His plans.

Share your experience now at
HungerNoMoreBook.com.

*"They remembered that God was their Rock,
that God Most High was their Redeemer."*
—Psalm 78:35

Despite God's goodness to Moses and the Israelites in the wilderness for 40 years, many of His people rebelled against Him. As a result, God allowed judgment to fall upon them on occasions, spurring God's people to return to the Lord. "They remembered that God was their Rock, that God Most High was their Redeemer."

The psalmist uses three names that highlight our understanding of the Lord. Their Rock was God as a solid foundation, One who could be trusted. "God Most High" emphasized the Lord's power above all other gods. "Redeemer" expressed a God who could save, both physically from Egyptian slavery as well as spiritually. Let us not reject God; let us remember His greatness today.

Share your experience now at
HungerNoMoreBook.com.

JULY 20

"Yet he was merciful; he forgave
their iniquities and did not destroy them."
—Psalm 78:38

Despite the many rejections by the Israelites after being rescued from Egypt, the Lord showed mercy. The psalmist noted, "Yet he was merciful; he forgave their iniquities and did not destroy them." They deserved death. They experienced mercy.

God's nature has not changed. In our lives, we deserve death for our sins, yet we experience the Lord's mercy. He has not destroyed us. We deserve judgment yet experience love. Despite our failings, He saves us by faith in our Lord Jesus Christ. Our salvation is not based on our good deeds, but upon His mercy. Let us never take this mercy for granted. May we rejoice in the Lord's great love. May we show His love to those we encounter today.

Share your experience now at
HungerNoMoreBook.com.

"David shepherded them with integrity of heart;
with skillful hands he led them."
—Psalm 78:72

An authentic spiritual leader requires two key abilities—integrity and ingenuity. David's life reflected both: "David shepherded them with integrity of heart; with skillful hands he led them." In his life, we find integrity first, skills second, yet both were important. God shaped his heart, and then shaped his mind. As a result, David was greatly used of God to lead many.

God still seeks such leaders today. Regardless of the size of the audience we lead, these two essentials must be developed. How is our integrity? What would God have us to sharpen in this area? How are continuing to learn and grow, improving our ability to improve the lives of others? God has saved us for service. Let us serve according to His ways.

Share your experience now at
HungerNoMoreBook.com.

JULY 22

"From generation to generation
we will proclaim your praise."
—Psalm 79:13

Music often divides people within a church. One group prefers more traditional music; another insists on newer songs; some want a bit of both. In the end, many people are often hurt and deep divisions are formed. This is clearly not God's desire. His focus has always been on His people praising Him regardless of generation, not according to their generation.

The psalmist expressed it this way: "From generation to generation we will proclaim your praise." His heart was on God rather than any person or group of people. When we follow this example, we will find ourselves less concerned with the style of our worship and more concerned with its substance. Let us focus on praising the Lord today, from generation to generation.

Share your experience now at
HungerNoMoreBook.com.

"Restore us, O God; make your face shine on us,
that we may be saved."
—Psalm 80:3

Salvation comes from God alone. There is no other source or point of distribution that will take us from earth to eternity with Him. Salvation is offered exclusively through the Lord. The psalmist recognized this truth and wrote, "Restore us, O God; make your face shine upon us, that we may be saved."

For our lives to change, God must act. Of course, we must obey Him. But unless He restores, we remain helpless and hopeless. This is why our utmost cry must be one of dependence on the Lord. Our human efforts do not move us one inch closer to Him. Yet in one move our God can awaken our hearts and invigorate our spirits anew. Let us seek God's restoration in our lives today. Let His face shine upon us.

Share your experience now at
HungerNoMoreBook.com.

"Return to us, God Almighty!
Look down from heaven and see!"
—Psalm 80:14

When our enemies triumph, we find ourselves turning to God for help. When Asaph found himself in this situation, he spoke directly to the Lord: "Return to us, God Almighty! Look down from heaven and see!" From his perspective, God had left him to fend for himself, resulting in painful defeat. "Where are you God?" was his cry.

We can certainly relate. There are many times we feel God has taken a vacation that has resulted in severe losses on our behalf. We find ourselves questioning or even demanding a response from the Lord. God understands our pain. He is always there ready to act. We need not doubt Him, only to trust Him even during our darkest of days.

Share your experience now at
HungerNoMoreBook.com.

"Revive us, and we will call on your name."
—Psalm 80:18

The Lord does not revive us simply for our own benefit. He revives us so we would praise Him: "Revive us, and we will call on your name." The Lord's renewal in our lives is not for our glory, but for His. When we recognize that He transforms us for His honor, it leads us to walk in humility and dependence.

Consider this: If we refuse to honor God in our lives, why should we expect Him to revive ours? God's desire is for servants who will faithfully serve His will. We must move beyond entitlement and embrace our role as God's dependents. Where He leads, we will follow. What He calls us to do must be answered with "Yes!" Let us fully follow Him today.

Share your experience now at
HungerNoMoreBook.com.

JULY 26

"In your distress you called and I rescued you."
—Psalm 81:7

God is our Rescuer. In each our lives, there are moments when we would have perished apart from God's intervention. "In your distress you called and I rescued you." The Lord both redeems us and then repeatedly rescues us in our times of need. His power is both our initial and ongoing source of strength.

The superheroes of today's media always seem to arrive just in time to save the planet from peril. Yet even the best superhero has limitations. He or she can never personally attend to each problem, nor can they walk alongside any one person without leaving out others. Our God walks with all of His children every moment of every day. He will be there in our moment of need.

Share your experience now at
HungerNoMoreBook.com.

"Defend the weak and the fatherless;
uphold the cause of the poor and the oppressed."
—Psalm 82:3

When we see those in need enduring suffering and mistreatment, it should cause us to cry out to God as the psalmist, "Defend the weak and the fatherless; uphold the cause of the poor and the oppressed." Rather than looking upon the poor with prejudice or disdain, we are to look at them as the Lord does—with compassion in action.

Even those who do not know the Lord often show great concern for the needy. Our love for God must result in a much deeper response than the average citizen. Let us intercede on behalf of our community's poor; let us participate as God leads to help be the answer to the prayers we offer. Our God is known for His compassion for the needy; let us be known for it as well.

Share your experience now at
HungerNoMoreBook.com.

JULY 28

"Let them know that you,
whose name is the LORD—
that you alone are the Most High over all the earth."
—Psalm 83:18

People cherish items that are unique. An exclusive, one-of-a-kind gift stands out even if it is smaller or less expensive than other gifts. Why? Because the item is uncommon and rare. What is true of the gifts we offer is far exceeded by the uniqueness of our God: "Let them know that you, who name is the LORD—that you alone are the Most High over all the earth."

The Lord is the only true God. Those who find Him find a rare gift indeed. When we connect with our Creator, we experience a joy unmatched anywhere else in all creation. This gift of God is one we not only enjoy ourselves; it is a gift we are to share with others.

Share your experience now at
HungerNoMoreBook.com.

"My soul yearns, even faints,
for the courts of the LORD;
my heart and my flesh cry out for the living God."
—Psalm 84:2

A re there ever times you feel so passionate for God that your body cannot contain the joy? The psalmist must have experienced this emotion when he wrote, "My soul yearns, even faints, for the courts of the LORD; my heart and flesh cry out for the living God." His desire was to worship God in the temple of the Lord.

While we do not constantly experience this level of emotion, there should be occasions when we do. At times, our Father blesses us with an intense joy that is centered on Him and His greatness. When we encounter such joy, let us be quick to offer praise back to God, thanking Him for a glimpse of the eternal bliss we will enjoy with Him forever..

Share your experience now at
HungerNoMoreBook.com.

July 30

"Better is one day in your courts
than a thousand elsewhere."
—Psalm 84:10

A moment in God's presence is better than an eternity of earthly riches without God. There is no greater satisfaction than to enjoy the presence of our Lord, the Creator of the heavens and earth. As the psalmist wrote, "Better is one day in your courts than a thousand elsewhere."

A day in the temple courts was a day spent in worship of God. This was no small commitment but rather a hefty obligation. Yet it was seen as better than a thousand days anywhere else. Why? What mattered was to be in the presence of God. Let our lives be marked by this same attitude. Let us be consumed by living moment by moment in the presence of God.

Share your experience now at
HungerNoMoreBook.com.

"For the LORD God is a sun and shield;
the LORD bestows favor and honor."
—Psalm 84:11

If God is on our side, nothing can stop us. When we walk according to His will, we may experience pain, but we will never experience defeat. "For the LORD God is a sun and shield; the LORD bestows favor and honor." Just as the sun brings a bright day and leads to a better harvest, so the Lord makes life of great benefit. As a shield protects from harm, God protects His people in times of need.

God's power serves as our power. In the life of a believer, His Spirit empowers us throughout the moments of our day. When enduring temptation or life's storms, we are never alone. He offers strength to meet each challenge. Let us look to His favor today.

Share your experience now at
HungerNoMoreBook.com.

*"Will you not revive us again,
that your people may rejoice in you?"*
—Psalm 85:6

When joy is lacking, momentum is missing. A task that would ordinarily take moments now seems impossible. Dishes stack up. Laundry piles high. Energy is fleeting. The psalmist understood this important connection between joy and passion when he wrote, "Will you not revive us again, that you people may rejoice in you?"

True revival is a work of God that leads to effective work by God's people. The psalmist longed for the Lord to provide this power that would restore joy and lead to changed lives. He held no answer in his own human abilities. Our goal today is to ask God for renewed passion rather than rely on our strength. Only then will we live with the godly joy He desires.

Share your experience now at
HungerNoMoreBook.com.

AUGUST 2

*"When I am in distress, I call to you,
because you answer me."*
—Psalm 86:7

Distress causes stress. An unexpected bill arrives. A negative medical diagnosis interrupts our lives. How do we handle the unanticipated interruptions of life? The psalmist turned to the Lord. Why? "When I am in distress, I call to you, because you answer me." He knew God would provide the answers he needed at just the right moment and in just the right way.

Our God is still in the business of answering our stressful situations. When we turn to Him, we find One who listens, who cares, and who responds. We may not understand why certain problems occur in our lives, but we understand who to run to when they do. Call to the Lord today. He will answer. He will respond.

Share your experience now at
HungerNoMoreBook.com.

AUGUST 3

*"Teach me your way, LORD, that I may rely
on your faithfulness; give me an undivided heart,
that I may fear your name."*
—Psalm 86:11

A hunger to learn is a hunger for faithfulness. The worshiper who longs to know God's Word, diligently reading for understanding, is the person whose heart truly seeks to honor the Lord with his or her life. David set an example in this area when he prayed, "Teach me your way, LORD, that I may rely on your faithfulness; give me an undivided heart, that I may fear your name."

Notice the clear parallels between learning and faithfulness, an undivided heart and worship. David's desire for further education was deeply connected with his devotion. We are called to live with passion and with understanding in our walk with God. Our Lord desires both. Let us live with hearts that long for God and His Word.

Share your experience now at
HungerNoMoreBook.com.

"He has founded his city on the holy mountain."
—Psalm 87:1

Jerusalem has long served as a city of sacred significance to God and His people. When David became king of Israel, Jerusalem served as the nation's capital. The temple was built there. The ark dwelt within its walls. The Messiah would come to this city and has promised to one day reign from a New Jerusalem forever. It is only fitting the psalmist would note, "He has founded his city on the holy mountain."

Ultimately, both Jerusalem and every good gift we have come from the Lord. When we acknowledge His gifts in praise to Him, we show gratitude for His blessings. How has the Lord blessed your life? Take a moment to thank Him for the great things He has done.

Share your experience now at
HungerNoMoreBook.com.

"Lord, you are the God who saves me;
day and night I cry out to you."
—Psalm 88:1

God is available every moment of every day. When we toss and turn deep into the night, He is there. During the frantic moments of our day, He is near. Better still, He longs for us to turn to Him in these moments: "LORD, you are the God who saves me; day and night I cry out to you."

Our Lord is always there, always listens, and always saves. No other god and no other source can make such a claim. There is no problem too big or issue too small for His concern. Even when we cannot express our hearts, He understands our needs. Let us cry out to Him today, whether morning, noon, or night. He is the God who saves us.

Share your experience now at
HungerNoMoreBook.com.

AUGUST 6

"In the morning my prayer comes before you."
—Psalm 88:13

We view morning as the beginning of the day. However, in Jewish culture, evening served as the start of the day. Sunset marked its beginning. Yet morning marked the time when life was most calm, before the business of the marketplace began. During this quiet, it was an ideal time to pray: "In the morning my prayer comes before you."

In fact, the temple ritual would have included an official morning prayer along with the daily sacrifice. This was much more than a few words during the morning commute; this was a dedicated, extended time of sacred reflection upon the greatness of the Lord. Let us turn to the Lord to start our day; let us share a sacred moment with Him.

Share your experience now at
HungerNoMoreBook.com.

*"I will sing of the LORD's great love forever;
with my mouth I will make your faithfulness
known through all generations."*
—Psalm 89:1

Music serves as one of the uniting cultural experience of each generation. Certain songs resonate deeply with each age within a cultural group in ways words cannot express. Perhaps this is why the psalmist wrote, "I will sing of the LORD's great love forever; with my mouth I will make your faithfulness known through all generations." His desire was to continually sing of God's love in a way that extended to future generations.

While this effort is a valiant one, there is also a sense in which believers will accomplish this in eternity with our Lord. There we will forever sing of His great love. Until then, our praises here serve as an opportunity to proclaim His greatness to all who will listen.

Share your experience now at
HungerNoMoreBook.com.

"For who in the skies above can compare with the LORD? Who is like the LORD among the heavenly beings?"
—Psalm 89:6

The era of Ethan had been exposed to the worldviews of outside cultures who worshiped a myriad of gods. It seemed there was a deity for every aspect of nature, whether the sea, stars, moon, or sky. As he gave praise to God, he rightly acknowledged, "For who in the skies above can compare with the LORD? Who is like the LORD among the heavenly beings?"

Ethan did not give credence to these other gods; instead, he belittled them as being of no comparison with the Lord. Only the God of Israel had performed miracles that had parted seas, controlled the powers of nature, and had even returned Israel to its land after years of exile. Let us worship only the Lord God today.

Share your experience now at
HungerNoMoreBook.com.

AUGUST 9

"Your arm is endowed with power;
your hand is strong, your right hand exalted."
—Psalm 89:13

Who formed the mountains and gave the oceans their boundaries? Who placed the stars in the sky? Who set the sun in its place to give us light? The Lord. His strength is unmatched, leading the psalmist to write, "Your arm is endowed with power; your hand is strong, your right hand exalted."

The One who holds the universe in His hands also holds our hand. He is both Creator and Counselor, revealing His great power while expressing His great love. Do we deserve His love? Did we do anything to earn it? Yet He cares for us as a celebrated child of His creation. Let us rejoice in His great power in our world and in our lives today.

Share your experience now at
HungerNoMoreBook.com.

AUGUST 10

"Blessed are those who have learned to acclaim you,
who walk in the light of your presence, LORD."
—Psalm 89:15

Life is different when we worship God. Our attitude no longer pursues self; it pursues our Savior. Yet it is in the unselfish act of praising God that we find personal blessing: "Blessed are those who have learned to acclaim you, who walk in the light of your presence, LORD." When we bless God, He blesses us. It is when we exchange our way for His way that we find a better way of life.

But a life of worship does not come easily. The temptation to turn our eyes from our Lord and onto other pursuits is a daily battle. In fact, each day, the struggle is moment by moment. Yet this passion for God is essential to our lives. Let us seek Him today.

Share your experience now at
HungerNoMoreBook.com.

AUGUST 11

"Indeed, our shield belongs to the LORD,
our king to the Holy One of Israel."
—Psalm 89:18

Have you ever stopped to consider that our nation's leaders serve under the authority of God? We may not always agree with their actions, yet His sovereign will ultimately controls their ways. The psalmist noted, "Indeed, our shield belongs to the LORD, our king to the Holy One of Israel.

Their "shield" referred to their strength. Their "king" represented the strength of the nation. In both cases, these concepts of strength belonged to the LORD. Today, take a moment to offer a special prayer on behalf of your governing leaders and the protection of your community. Ask the Lord for wisdom among those who lead where you live. May God be the strength that guides their lives and yours this day.

Share your experience now at
HungerNoMoreBook.com.

*"Lord, you have been our dwelling place
throughout all generations."*
—Psalm 90:1

Who was the oldest person to write one of the Psalms? As far as we know, the answer is Moses. The same man who met with God to receive the Ten Commandments also penned these words: "Lord, you have been our dwelling place throughout all generations." Moses acknowledged that we live because of Him and are to live for Him. Why? For God is the Creator of all things.

Further, this promise applied "throughout all generations." Still today, our Lord is to be revered and feared. We are to seek Him and serve Him. There is no point at which living for God becomes irrelevant or unnecessary, antiquated or outdated. He is deserving of our full allegiance and devotion, both now and forevermore.

Share your experience now at
HungerNoMoreBook.com.

> *"Teach us to number our days,*
> *that we may gain a heart of wisdom."*
> —Psalm 90:12

Life is short. The longer we live, the faster the years pass. What we once counted in days, we now count in years. Perhaps this is why Moses wrote, "Teach us to number our days, that we may gain a heart of wisdom." When we realize the shortness of life, we begin to see the importance of makeing every moment count. Moses called such a realization part of a heart of wisdom.

Are you seeking to live each moment to its fullest? This is our calling and goal. God desires a full devotion to Him, including our use of time. To do so, we must make two decisions. First, what must I do less? Second, what must I do more? Let us make every moment count.

Share your experience now at
HungerNoMoreBook.com.

"Satisfy us in the morning with your unfailing love,
that we may sing for joy and be glad all our days."
—Psalm 90:14

For 40 years in the wilderness, Moses and the Israelites woke up to manna. God supernaturally provided this daily bread to meet their physical needs. Yet Moses preferred one thing each morning even above food: "Satisfy us in the morning with your unfailing love, that we may sing for joy and be glad all our days."

Love was of utmost important to Moses. Such affection would cause him to sing with joy throughout the day. The same baby spared from death in a basket built by a mother's love later sustained himself with the perfect love only God could provide. Let us likewise find joy in the Lord's love. Let it cause us to sing with gladness all our days.

Share your experience now at
HungerNoMoreBook.com.

AUGUST 15

"Whoever dwells in the shelter of the Most High will rest in the shadow of the Almighty."
—Psalm 91:1

Those who live close to God find rest. When people ask how we are doing, a common response is, "Staying busy." This is usually seen as a good thing, a sign of productiveness and importance. Yet the psalmist offers an alternative view of God's desire for our lives: "Whoever dwells in the shelter of the Most High will rest in the shadow of the Almighty."

To be busy is not wrong; to live busy is. Despite the pace of our schedule, our Lord calls us to rest next to Him, in His shadow. The other option is to move forward in our own power, where we find both a hectic schedule and life. God offers us rest. We need only accept His invitation.

Share your experience now at
HungerNoMoreBook.com.

AUGUST 16

"He will call on me, and I will answer him;
I will be with him in trouble."
—Psalm 91:15

When we find ourselves in trouble, we tend to run from God. Even the first human sin led to Adam and Eve hiding from the Lord in the garden. Rather than seek His fellowship, they sought to escape His presence. Our weaknesses often cause us shame, leading us to flee rather than cling to God.

Yet our Father wants His children to run to Him in times of trouble: "He will call on me, and I will answer him; I will be with him in trouble." God wants to be "with us" during our difficult times. We dare not and cannot run from God. Let us not run from Him; let us run to Him. Let us call to Him and look for His answer.

Share your experience now at
HungerNoMoreBook.com.

"For you make me glad by your deeds, LORD;
I sing for joy at what your hands have done."
—Psalm 92:4

God's answers to our needs lead us to adore God for His deeds. When He shows up by His mighty hand, we cannot help but lift up our hands in praise. The psalmist expressed it another way: "For you make me glad by your deeds, LORD; I sing for joy at what your hands have done."

How has God answered your prayers in recent days? In what areas of life has the Lord provided for your needs? Count the ways and give Him praise. Like a loving Father, our Lord enjoys the adoration of His children. God is pleased with the gratitude of His little ones. Let us find joy in His answers; let us sing for joy to the One who has answered.

Share your experience now at
HungerNoMoreBook.com.

*"The LORD is upright; he is my Rock,
and there is no wickedness in him."*
—Psalm 92:15

Tainted water tastes impure. Even the smallest amount of change can affect both the taste and quality of the substance. The same is true in our lives; the smallest of sins makes us impure; not one of us is perfect in all our ways. Only God exists without fault: "The LORD is upright; he is my Rock, and there is no wickedness in him."

Because God is perfect, we can look to Him for a perfect answer to our every need. We may not understand all of His ways, but we can understand His way is perfect. All of our insufficiencies and insecurities find their fullness in His perfect sufficiency. Let us not live trying to be "good enough." Let us live dependent upon God.

Share your experience now at
HungerNoMoreBook.com.

"The LORD reigns, he is robed in majesty; the LORD is robed in majesty and armed with strength."
—Psalm 93:1

The Psalms often depict God as a King. He is the One who reigns over all. His wonder is unmatched, His might unparalleled. The psalmist declares, "The LORD reigns, he is robed in majesty . . . and armed with strength."

His reign includes the entire universe. Not one inch of creation exists outside His realm. His majesty includes the greatest creations we can imagine—the constellations in the sky and even the planets of our solar system and beyond. His strength can shakes mountains and control the waves of the sea. The God we serve holds the power to solve any problem we face. We are blessed to serve as citizens in His kingdom. Let us worship and serve Him as King this day.

Share your experience now at
HungerNoMoreBook.com.

*"Does he who fashioned the ear not hear?
Does he who formed the eye not see?"*
—Psalm 94:9

We can never hide from God. He knows our every breath and our every heartbeat. He understands our every thought before we even think it. It is futile to cover up ours sins from Him: "Does he who fashioned the ear not hear? Does he who formed the eye not see?" He hears all, sees all, and knows all.

Rather than hide from the Lord, we are called to confess our failures to Him. When we sin, we turn to Him for mercy. Running away from God only wears us out. Running to God renews our strength. Let us bring all our concerns before Him. Let us cast before Him every care. His desire is to help us move forward, relying upon His strength to live this day.

Share your experience now at
HungerNoMoreBook.com.

August 21

"The LORD has become my fortress,
and my God the rock in whom I take refuge."
—Psalm 94:22

Fortress. Rock. Refuge. These three words are often mentioned together in the Psalms in connection with God: "The LORD has become my fortress, and my God the rock in whom I take refuge." In a time and place in which war was common, issues related to safety were foremost on the minds of many citizens. To encourage hearers to see the Lord as their place of safety pointed to a power beyond physical strength to supply safety.

God's people were sure to understand this psalm. The Lord had often saved Israel despite overwhelming odds. Even today, we can look to how God has worked throughout history to reveal how He can work in our story. Let us count on Him for our security today.

Share your experience now at
HungerNoMoreBook.com.

August 22

"Come, let us sing for joy to the LORD."
—Psalm 95:1

Music can serve as a tremendous encouragement. The right song at the right time can be transforming to even the most sensitive situations. In fact, during the important events of life, such as a wedding or a funeral, much focus is given to the selection and performance of the exact music that will take place.

When the psalmist wrote, "Come, let us sing for joy to the LORD," it served to motivate those gathered to join together in a song of praise to God. This was not a solemn occasion, but a time for joy. Let us use music in our lives to express our hearts for our Creator. May we sing for joy to Him today, encouraging others to join us in praise.

Share your experience now at
HungerNoMoreBook.com.

*"Come, let us bow down in worship,
let us kneel before the LORD our Maker."*
—Psalm 95:6

Bowing down serves as a sign of reverence. Still today, some Eastern cultures use bowing to greet one another. The deeper a person bows, the more respect it shows. A close friend may receive a small tip of the head; a community leader would receive a full bow, extending honor to one in a position of power.

The idea of bowing is important in our worship of God as well: "Come, let us bow down in worship, let us kneel before the LORD our Maker." Both bowing and kneeling, we are called to show utmost respect to our King. This attitude can be reflected in both our posture and in our hearts. We dare not come to Him as an equal; we worship Him as Lord.

Share your experience now at
HungerNoMoreBook.com.

AUGUST 24

*"Declare his glory among the nations,
his marvelous deeds among all peoples."*
—Psalm 96:3

God's greatness is not intended to be a secret. The psalmist sang, "Declare his glory among the nations, his marvelous deeds among all peoples." Our goal is to bring the love of our Lord to every person in every place on the planet. There is no location too remote or too far removed from our experience that we should not endeavor to bring them the same love of God we experience.

We know this, yet our lives often do not reflect the urgency of this calling. Those across the street and across the sea must hear the good news available through the Messiah, Jesus Christ. Let us pray and live today to help those near and far experience the love of our Lord.

Share your experience now at
HungerNoMoreBook.com.

249

AUGUST 25

*"Worship the LORD in the splendor of his holiness;
tremble before him, all the earth."*
—Psalm 96:9

God is holy. Unless He had made a way, there would be no way for us to come near to Him. The psalmist wrote, "Worship the LORD in the splendor of his holiness; tremble before him, all the earth." Worship here was connected with trembling. To come before God was a fearful endeavor.

We often fail to consider the awesome holiness of God when we come to Him in prayer. Though we can approach Him at any time, it is not an experience to be taken lightly. At times, it would even be appropriate to tremble at the thought of worshiping the Creator of all the earth. Let us live mindful of His perfect holiness today. Let us come before Him with great reverence.

Share your experience now at
HungerNoMoreBook.com.

*"For you, LORD, are the Most High over
all the earth; you are exalted far above all gods."*
—Psalm 97:9

God has no equal. Despite the claims of other religions, there is only One who created the earth and everything on it: "For you, LORD, are the Most High over all the earth; you are exalted far above all gods." What other god or goddess created the plants, the animals, the skies, the seas, or human life? There is none! Only the Lord.

This is a matter of both truth and worship. When we acknowledge the Lord as the only God, it leads us to worship Him as well. We don't merely proclaim God is One; we praise our one God, rejecting worship of any and all other powers. Let us declare His greatness today; He alone is worthy of worship.

Share your experience now at
HungerNoMoreBook.com.

*"Sing to the LORD a new song,
for he has done marvelous things."*
—Psalm 98:1

Most people prefer what is new. The latest is considered the greatest, whether a new car, a new home, or new clothing. Perhaps this attitude existed in the time of the psalmist as well, who wrote, "Sing to the LORD a new song, for he has done marvelous things." The great works of God were to lead to singing a new song to God, one uniquely developed to worship Him in a fresh way.

Have you ever written a song? Even if no one else ever reads it, perhaps today would be the time to write down some of your own feelings toward the Lord. Speak of His great works. Tell of what He has done. Today, sing to the Lord a new song in your life.

Share your experience now at
HungerNoMoreBook.com.

"Let them praise your great
and awesome name—he is holy."
—Psalm 99:3

Not only is God to be worshipped—even His Name is to be praised: "Let them praise you great and awesome name—he is holy." Everything about the Lord is perfect, including His Name. A quick look at the variety of names used for God in the Bible reveals that each shares a unique aspect of His greatness.

Adonai focuses on His power as Lord. Yahweh was the unspoken name of God because it was considered so holy. Shepherd refers to God as the One who guides us. God is also called our Healer, the One who can remove our sickness or pain. If you desire a fresh experience with God today, take a moment to look at the greatness of His many names.

Share your experience now at
HungerNoMoreBook.com.

"Worship the LORD with gladness;
come before him with joyful songs."
—Psalm 100:2

A defining attitude of one who worships God is joy. The psalmist wrote, "Worship the LORD with gladness; come before him with joyful songs." Those who love God enjoy times of gladness for they have discovered the joy of knowing the Lord.

The Apostle Peter would later write that His Lord Jesus gave him "inexpressible, glorious joy" (1 Peter 1:8). Salvation in Jesus had given both purpose and gladness to his life. Still today, those who know Christ find joy despite their circumstances. We may face difficult challenges today, yet the Lord is with us. Because of this, we can walk with joy through even the worst of situations. Today, worship the Lord with gladness. Offer Him songs of joy.

Share your experience now at
HungerNoMoreBook.com.

"It is he who made us, and we are his."
—Psalm 100:3

God has both created us and owns us. He has not built us to sell or to give to another. We are His children. We are made in His image for His purposes. "It is he who made us, and we are his."

So often, we base our self-worth on the opinions of others. But they do not own us, did not create us, nor do they usually know us intimately. But our Lord does. He created us for His glory. When we look at a consumer product, there is often a label that lists where it was made. But not on people. We have been made by God and for God. Let us live for His glory in our lives today.

Share your experience now at
HungerNoMoreBook.com.

"We are his people, the sheep of his pasture."
—Psalm 100:3

God often compares His people to sheep in Scripture. Since many of the Bible's original readers were shepherds or worked in agriculture, this analogy made sense. A good shepherd cared for his or her animals, provided for them, and even loved them.

When God calls us His sheep, He reveals much about both Himself and His people. He is the leader, the provider, and protector. We are the followers, the needy, and the vulnerable. Our lives are completely in His hands. Rather than trusting in our own power, we must count on His strength to meet our needs each day. As shepherd, God shows His love by watching out for us and meeting our every need. He will never leave us; we are His sheep.

Share your experience now at
HungerNoMoreBook.com.

*"Enter his gates with thanksgiving
and his courts with praise."*
—Psalm 100:4

We begin our prayers with thanksgiving, not complaining. The psalmist sets the example in his words, "Enter his gates with thanksgiving and his courts with praise." We come to God with our problems, but we begin with our praise.

Gates present a picture of an entry or starting point. Courtyards naturally followed in many Jewish buildings, including the temple. This reminder from architecture presents the ideal order to our worship. Praise, then petition. Adoration, then asking. When we begin with a heart of generosity, we are also likely to offer our requests according to God's will and in God's way. Let us worship our heavenly Father today with a soul that expresses gratitude. Let our prayer overflow in ceaseless praise.

Share your experience now at
HungerNoMoreBook.com.

"For the LORD is good and his love endures forever;
his faithfulness continues through all generations."
—Psalm 100:5

We serve a good God. He is not a Deity who stands above waiting to attack, nor a tyrant who seeks to punish for no reason. He is full of love, and is love. As the psalmist declared, "For the LORD is good and his love endures forever; his faithfulness continues through all generations."

A proper view of God provides a proper context for worship. When we better understand our Lord's perfect goodness, love, and faithfulness, we stand in awe of His greatness. Rather than wrongful attitudes that lead us to avoid Him or speak poorly of His name, we live in reverence. We serve from an overflow of joy, not an abundance of guilt. The Lord is good and longs for our good.

Share your experience now at
HungerNoMoreBook.com.

SEPTEMBER 3

*"I will conduct the affairs of my house
with a blameless heart."*
—Psalm 101:2

Integrity is both a decision and a process. We do not become men or women of integrity until after we choose to live with integrity. This is the commitment spoken of by David when he wrote, "I will conduct the affairs of my house with a blameless heart." He sought to worship God through the way he treated those around him.

The same principle remains true in our lives. A heart that seeks to worship God also seeks to live by God's principles in everyday life. Worship is not a Sunday-only activity; it is a 24/7 responsibility. Let us honor our Lord through the way we live our lives today, with every interaction and every fiber of our being.

Share your experience now at
HungerNoMoreBook.com.

*"Do not hide your face from me
when I am in distress."*
—Psalm 102:2

We can endure anything in this life—but only with God by our side. During life's toughest battles, people will disappoint and our human inventions will lack the ability to bring success. Only if the Lord is near will we survive. Our attitude in these times must reflect that of the psalmist who cried, "Do not hide your face from me when I am in distress."

The temptation is great to believe God has turned against us when life turns upside down. Yet the opposite is true. When we fall to our lowest, the Lord Most High holds us in His arms. We can call out to Him, trusting He will never let us drop from the safety of His protection.

Share your experience now at
HungerNoMoreBook.com.

*"You remain the same,
and your years will never end."*
—Psalm 102:27

God is both unchanging and eternal. These two attributes exist intertwined in a perfection available only to our Lord: "You remain the same, and your years will never end." As a result, we can trust Him to fulfill every promise. We can count on Him to right every wrong. He will never disappear nor fail.

Our Lord's power offers an unchanging comfort for our ever-changing lives. Though our days shift like the wind and our lives are but a few years, we can connect with the power of One who transcends our physical limitations. With His strength, we stand ready to confront the challenges of life. With His might, we have a power that will carry us through our earthly existence and all eternity.

Share your experience now at
HungerNoMoreBook.com.

SEPTEMBER 6

"Praise the LORD, my soul;
all my inmost being, praise his holy name."
—Psalm 103:1

Coaches regularly challenge their athletes to give their all on the field. The goal is to give one hundred percent effort. What is true in the athletic realm is much truer in the spiritual realm. Our worship of God is not a part of our lives; worship is our lives: "Praise the LORD, my soul; all my inmost being, praise his holy name."

The best athletes are those with the greatest passion. Their love for the game inspires teammates and fans, bringing a heightened level of energy to all. Likewise, our all-out pursuit of God can inspire those around us. More importantly, it is God's desire that we love Him with all our heart. Let us worship Him with all our being today.

Share your experience now at
HungerNoMoreBook.com.

September 7

"The LORD works righteousness and justice
for all the oppressed."
—Psalm 103:6

When we see injustice, we feel compelled to help. From the car on the side of the road to famine on the other side of the planet, those in need pull at our hearts. Even in our best moments, we realize our efforts fall far short of our desire to help. There are more needs than hours in the day; more problems than resources to solve them.

Yet the Lord sees these problems even much more clearly than we do. He not only sees, He intervenes in ways that only He can: "The LORD works righteousness and justice for all the oppressed." What we cannot do, He can. Let us serve those in need, knowing God likewise sees and acts to provide justice to the oppressed.

Share your experience now at
HungerNoMoreBook.com.

"The LORD is compassionate and gracious,
slow to anger, abounding in love."
—Psalm 103:8

Compassion is passion to help meet a need. This longing is not only a human desire, but one that originates with the Lord: "The LORD is compassionate and gracious, slow to anger, abounding in love."

The grace we need to live each day flows from our heavenly Father like a flood. It is not a trickle. When we fall, He does not treat us as our sins deserve. He extends grace—the same grace a loving father showers upon his child. Let us not see God as an angry tyrant, but as a compassionate King. He cares for us, offers us grace, and abounds in love. We are called to follow His pattern in these areas. Let us offer compassion and grace today.

Share your experience now at
HungerNoMoreBook.com.

*"As far as the east is from the west,
so far has he removed our transgressions from us."*
—Psalm 103:12

When God forgives our sins, He doesn't forget them; He removes them. And He doesn't just move them to the corner of the room for another day: "As far as the east is from the west, so far has he removed our transgression from us." God's forgiveness equals complete removal. Our forgiven sins cease to exist.

As a result, we receive the blessing to begin new lives, free from the guilt of sin and liberated to live in the joy the Lord offers. Yet though this forgiveness is freely given, it is not cheap. This forgiveness ultimately cost the Son of God His life upon the cross. Let us offer praise for His forgiveness. Let us share His offer of forgiveness to others today.

Share your experience now at
HungerNoMoreBook.com.

"As a father has compassion on his children,
so the LORD has compassion on those who fear him."
—Psalm 103:13

David's father was known as a righteous man. In raising David, Jesse would have shown compassion on several occasions. We are not given details, but maybe Jesse helped David clean a cut on David's knee. Maybe he helped his son track down lost sheep. Whatever it was, we know David saw it as a positive experience that influenced how he communicated the compassion of God.

Years later, David would write, "As a father has compassion on his children, so the LORD has compassion on those who fear him." Just as David experienced the care of his dad, he recognized a similar trait in his walk with God. Our heavenly Father loves us more than we could ever know.

Share your experience now at
HungerNoMoreBook.com.

September 11

*"From everlasting to everlasting
the LORD's love is with those who fear him,
and his righteousness with their children's children."*
—Psalm 103:17

When we follow the Lord, His love extends to others beyond us. Our family members are influenced as well: "The LORD's love is with those who fear him, and his righteousness with their children's children." The relationship we have with God will even influence our grandchildren!

Why is this? Our godly lives can impact our children, who in turn are likely to live for God when raising their own children. The actions you take today not only impact you; they influence generations. Every matter matters for eternity. Let us live today for the Lord. Our decisions will make a difference for those we meet today; they will also make a difference for those yet to be born in the generations to come.

Share your experience now at
HungerNoMoreBook.com.

September 12

"The LORD has established his throne in heaven,
and his kingdom rules over all."
—Psalm 103:19

Kings rule kingdoms within certain borders. There are limits to their power. But not with the Lord. As King of kings, His power knows no boundaries. "The LORD has established his throne in heaven, and his kingdom rules over all."

The Jewish view of God's throne in heaven was as a seat of authority above all where He could see all. From one side of the earth to the other, the King could watch over His kingdom and maintain His rule. He sees and knows all we will experience today. We have no need to worry; our King reigns over all. The One who controls the universe will direct our paths today. Let us live as faithful servants to our King today.

Share your experience now at
HungerNoMoreBook.com.

SEPTEMBER 13

"LORD my God, you are very great;
you are clothed with splendor and majesty."
—Psalm 104:1

We don't often think of God's clothes, but one psalmist speaks of what our Lord wears: "LORD, my God, you are very great; you are clothed with splendor and majesty." Though poetic in nature, the psalmist uses the concept of clothing to highlight the beauty of our Lord. He wears the clothing of a King. He dons the wardrobe of greatness.

In our culture, clothing is often viewed as a symbol of status or popularity. The more expensive the clothing, the more attention we give. Ancient kings often wore exquisite robes to display their power in this way, but no king's glory compares to God. His power transcends all earthly powers. His power will strengthen us through the experiences we face today.

Share your experience now at
HungerNoMoreBook.com.

"How many are your works, LORD! In wisdom you made them all; the earth is full of your creatures."
—Psalm 104:24

Scientists often find themselves in awe at the complexity of the created world. Even the myriad parts of a single human cell continue to baffle our world's most intelligent scholars. When we take a serious look at the creation around us, we find ourselves nearly speechless. As the psalmist wrote, "How many are your works, LORD! In wisdom you made them all; the earth is full of your creatures."

We cannot even count the exact number of animals and plants on our planet, much less can we understand them all. Only the power of a perfect, loving Creator could provide such an amazing existence. Let us look at the creation around us today and give praise. Let us say, "How many are your works, LORD!"

Share your experience now at
HungerNoMoreBook.com.

*"All creatures look to you
to give them their food at the proper time."*
—Psalm 104:27

Birds don't make a grocery list. You will never find a zebra trying to decide which restaurant to choose. Their menu comes from God. "All creatures look to you to give them their food at the proper time." Animals don't plant crops; they eat from what God provides.

This simple observation offers deep insight for those willing to listen. Just as God's other creations count on Him for sustenance, so we also find ourselves wholly dependent upon God to meet our needs. We may think we plan our meals, but God provides them. Let us live thankful for His provision. Let us not take what we eat for granted; let us view our meals as an opportunity to give our Lord praise.

Share your experience now at
HungerNoMoreBook.com.

SEPTEMBER 16

"May the glory of the LORD endure forever;
may the LORD rejoice in his works."
—Psalm 104:31

Our earthly existence has one major problem—it's temporary. Even the longest of us will live but a century, a mere speck in the timeline of world history. Yet God's power extends beyond our limits: "May the glory of the LORD endure forever; may the LORD rejoice in his works." Time is not an issue for Him; He created it.

When we recognize our life's length in comparison with God's eternal glory, our response is to be one of praise. We praise Him now, knowing that our faith in Him offers us a future eternity in His presence. Our knees may fail and our eyesight may fade in this life, but not with God. Our eternal Father offers us an eternal home with Him.

Share your experience now at
HungerNoMoreBook.com.

"I will sing praise to my God as long as I live."
—Psalm 104:33

It is easy to praise God when life is going well. If there is money in the bank and gas in the tank, thankfulness comes easily. It's when life takes a turn for the worst that our faith finds its truest test. Yet our goal is to say with the psalmist, "I will sing praise to my God as long as I live."

When life's struggles press in, will we continue to praise Him? When we walk through the dark seasons of life, will we continue to honor God? Let us choose now how we will respond then. Let us resolve not to stray during times of struggle. Let us choose to praise God today, tomorrow, and beyond. Let us give praise to God as long as we live.

Share your experience now at
HungerNoMoreBook.com.

*"May my meditation be pleasing to him,
as I rejoice in the LORD."*
—Psalm 104:34

God not only wants us to pray to Him; He desires for us to rejoice in Him. The psalmist wrote, "May my meditation be pleasing to him, as I rejoice in the LORD." We are called to both meditate and to celebrate.

In fact, meditation often leads to celebration. When we reflect on the greatness of God and what He has done in our lives, our hearts overflow with joy. We cannot help but to express thanks for His many expressions of provision in our times of need. If we were to list the works of the Lord, our writing would never end. Let our lives focus on the Lord today, both in remembering what He has done and rejoicing as a result.

Share your experience now at
HungerNoMoreBook.com.

*"Give praise to the LORD, proclaim his name;
make known among the nations what he has done."*
—Psalm 105:1

We praise God by sharing Him. While there are many ways to praise the Lord, the psalmist makes clear that evangelism can powerfully serve as an act of worship: "Give praise to the LORD, proclaim his name; make known among the nations what he has done." Our worship of God and our witness for God stand intimately connected.

When we fail to share our faith, what does it say about our view of the Lord? The greater we see God, the more we long to share Him. He is not an optional conversation topic; He is the topic of conversation. If He matters most, God will come up the most in our conversations. Let us praise God and proclaim Him to others today.

Share your experience now at
HungerNoMoreBook.com.

September 20

"Look to the LORD and his strength;
seek his face always."
—Psalm 105:4

When we are weak, our God is strong. We need not look in the mirror at our weaknesses; we need instead to look to the face of our Father: "Look to the LORD and his strength; seek his face always." Despite our limitations, we serve One without limitations. Where we lack power, He shows His power. When we face problems, we look to His face.

With God's power within us, we find an inner-power to meet any situation. His power empowers us. There is no foe too strong nor problem too difficult. The Creator of all things helps us through every situation. He will not let us fall from His grip. His hand holds us through each day. We need only seek His face.

Share your experience now at
HungerNoMoreBook.com.

SEPTEMBER 21

"Remember the wonders he has done."
—Psalm 105:5

Remembering is an act of worship. When we reflect upon God's past faithfulness, we experience God anew. In observing His past greatness, we find a present joy in His greatness. He has rescued us from every situation; His faithfulness has kept us through each trial. His mercies are new every morning.

The cost of remembering is patience. When we rush through our day, we forget the Lord's past answers and focus on present problems. Let us pause to refocus on what God has done before we concentrate on what He would have us to do today. How has God worked in your life? Rejoice in it. You'll find yourself better prepared to face today's agenda and more passionate in your walk with God.

Share your experience now at
HungerNoMoreBook.com.

*"He brought out his people with rejoicing,
his chosen ones with shouts of joy."*
—Psalm 105:43

When Moses led the Israelites out of their slavery in Egypt, their response was joy. They had served in bondage. Now they were free. In their freedom, the people gave praise to the Lord: "He brought out his people with rejoicing, his chosen ones with shouts of joy." Their rescue was reason to rejoice.

The same is true in our lives. When the Lord answers our cries, our response is to be one of praise. We dare not ask the Lord for an answer, receive it, then neglect Him. Rather, we seek His response to our needs then respond to Him in praise. He loves us and longs to care for our needs. Let us likewise love Him and long to give Him our praise.

Share your experience now at
HungerNoMoreBook.com.

*"Give thanks to the LORD, for he is good;
his love endures forever."*
—Psalm 106:1

Thankfulness is both an attitude and a habit. We choose to give thanks to God and we make a habit of thanking Him as a result. It is sometimes a natural response, but not always. Therefore, the psalmist calls us to, "Give thanks to the LORD, for he is good; his love endures forever."

As if we need another reason to give thanks to God, the psalmist reminds us that the Lord's love is eternal and without end. Our Father's concern for us will never cease; His compassion will never end. We can trust Him with our entire being, for He created our entire being. Let us give thanks to the Lord. Let it be our attitude and our habit to say, "Thank-You, God!"

Share your experience now at
HungerNoMoreBook.com.

SEPTEMBER 24

"Blessed are those who act justly,
who always do what is right."
—Psalm 106:3

God blesses obedience. He may not grant riches or freedom from harm to those who live righteous lives, but the Lord does promise blessing: "Blessed are those who act justly, who always do what is right." He cares about the condition of our hearts and the actions of our lives.

We are called to obey out of our love for our heavenly Father. Just as a child desires to please his or her loving father, so we are to seek to please God through our everyday thoughts, words, and actions. Let us live today mindful to do what is right not for the approval of others, but out of our love for God. Our godly obedience brings joy to the heart of our heavenly Father.

Share your experience now at
HungerNoMoreBook.com.

"He saved them for his name's sake,
to make his mighty power known."
—Psalm 106:8

God's actions make His power known. When He rescued His people from Pharaoh in Egypt, "He saved them for his name's sake, to make his mighty power known." He could have led His people out through another way, yet He chose a series of supernatural occurrences that led those watching to clearly note that this rescue was a work of God.

We find this concept at work in our own lives as well. Our Lord often chooses to act in ways that make it very clear that He is the One providing the answer. Our solution is not one we would or could choose. The path is not one we would or could create. God's unusual answers are His way of showing His supernatural power.

Share your experience now at
HungerNoMoreBook.com.

SEPTEMBER 26

"He took note of their distress
when he heard their cry."
—Psalm 106:44

When we endure hardship, we find ourselves crying out to God. Is He there? Is He concerned with our problems? According to Scripture He is and He does: "He took note of their distress when he heard their cry." God pays attention when we call to Him. Our cries become His cries. He takes a personal interest in the concerns of His children.

This psalm goes on to point out that God is not only interested but also intercedes. When the time is right, His response appears. He shows His love through His answers, His grace, and His forgiveness. If you're hurting, cry out to Him. He's taking notes. He will answer with the perfect response of a loving Father looking out for His child.

Share your experience now at
HungerNoMoreBook.com.

*"Praise be to the LORD, the God of Israel,
from everlasting to everlasting."*
—Psalm 106:48

God has no beginning and no end. Time does not control Him for He created time. He is never in a hurry and never late. Our Lord's timing is always right on time. The psalmist noted, "Praise be to the LORD, the God of Israel, from everlasting to everlasting." He has been Israel's God from eternity past and will be for eternity future, just as He is for us.

Since God exists outside of time, He also has all of the time He needs to personally act in each of our lives. There is never a rush to the next meeting or next message. His agenda is always clear. We need not come to God worried whether He can fit us into His schedule.

Share your experience now at
HungerNoMoreBook.com.

SEPTEMBER 28

"Give thanks to the LORD, for he is good;
his love endures forever."
—Psalm 107:1

One reason we give thanks to God is for His goodness. He not only does good, He *is* good. We can count on Him to never sin, never falter, and never fail. We can, "Give thanks to the LORD, for he is good; his love endures forever." We glorify God for His goodness; we praise Him for His perfection.

As a good God, He offers perfect love. We may fail Him, but He will never fail us. There is never a moment when God chooses no longer to love us. In fact, He loved us before the creation of time, and He will love us for all eternity. Let us respond with a heart of love for Him. Let us live a life of thanks.

Share your experience now at
HungerNoMoreBook.com.

"Let the redeemed of the LORD tell their story."
—Psalm 107:2

The story of God's work in our lives is worth telling. In fact, the psalmist wrote, "Let the redeemed of the LORD tell their story." He called hearers to share the narrative God has placed in our hearts with others. Our redemption is not a list of regulations; it is a story of salvation, a chronicle of our Father's wondrous compassion.

What is the story of God's redemption in your life? Tell it. Write it down. Share it. In fact, your life is a story—one authored by the Author of life to be read by a world in need of redemption. Tell your story today, through your words and your actions. Let others see and hear the Lord's redemption through you.

Share your experience now at
HungerNoMoreBook.com.

"They cried out to the LORD in their trouble,
and he delivered them from their distress."
—Psalm 107:6

Trouble is an invitation to prayer. When life falls apart, we can seek to respond in our own strength or to turn to the strength of the Lord. Yet only God can adequately handle the problems we face. When God's people encountered impossible obstacles, "They cried out to the LORD in their trouble, and he delivered them from their distress."

Packages don't jump out of our hands and onto delivery trucks. We must send them with a label to the proper address. Likewise, God doesn't usually answer our requests until we first come to Him in prayer with our pleas. In our trouble, we address our needs to God. We can always count on Him to deliver when we run to Him.

Share your experience now at
HungerNoMoreBook.com.

*"He satisfies the thirsty
and fills the hungry with good things."*
—Psalm 107:9

God perfectly answers our needs and answers our needs perfectly. As the psalmist wrote, "He satisfies the thirsty and fills the hungry with good things." The Lord could provide only the minimum requirements to sustain life, yet He often provides above and beyond what is necessary. Why? Because of His love.

A father's love will cause him to travel to great lengths to find the perfect gift for his children. Our heavenly Father's love causes Him to answer our needs perfectly, not just adequately. When we experience His love, it causes our love to increase for Him. May we worship our Father for His great gifts to us. Let us thank Him for satisfying our thirst and hunger with good things.

Share your experience now at
HungerNoMoreBook.com.

October 2

"Then they cried to the LORD in their trouble,
and he saved them from their distress."
—Psalm 107:19

To cry out to the Lord admits our neediness. Try as we may to answer our own problems in our own strength, we soon discover only the Lord's help will suffice: "Then they cried out to the LORD in their trouble, and he saved them from their distress." Trouble had come, God's people had cried out, and He chose to save them.

This appears to serve as God's order for our lives as well. God does not remove us from all harm; He uses harm to move us closer to Him. We call to Him, acknowledging the Lord as our only hope. He rescues us, proving Himself strong. Let us not fear our circumstances, but our Lord. Let us trust Him in times of trouble.

Share your experience now at
HungerNoMoreBook.com.

October 3

"Let the one who is wise heed these LORD."
—Psalm 107:43

Those who are wise thank God for what He has done. The unwise complain about what He has not done. As the psalmist wrote, "Let the one who is wise heed these things and ponder the loving deeds of the LORD." Reflection is an act of wisdom. When we look back at God's actions in our lives, we find a series of loving works that reveal the heart of our caring heavenly Father.

Godly wisdom includes not only reflection; it also includes evaluation. When we see what God has done for us, it can cause us to change how we live for Him. How can we serve Him better? How can we increase in our love for Him and for others today?

Share your experience now at
HungerNoMoreBook.com.

"Be exalted, O God, above the heavens;
let your glory be over all the earth."
—Psalm 108:5

A right view of God precedes proper worship of God. When we realize His greatness over all, we find ourselves honoring Him above all. David sang such words upon His understanding of the Lord's greatness: "Be exalted, O God, above the heavens; let your glory be over all the earth."

To ask for God to be exalted is proclaim Him as higher than all. To speak of His glory over all the earth is to ask for all people to see the Lord as David saw Him—as the all-powerful Creator. May we seek to increase our view of the Lord that we may increase our worship of the Lord. Let us lift Him up anew this day.

Share your experience now at
HungerNoMoreBook.com.

October 5

"My God, whom I praise, do not remain silent."
—Psalm 109:1

When we fail to hear from God, how are we to respond? We do not pout; we praise. The psalmist pleaded, "My God, whom I praise, do not remain silent." God is there even when we cannot discern His voice amidst the noise in our lives. Our goal is to praise Him even when He seems distant and far away.

It is then that we often hear from God most clearly. During the storms of life, booming thunder may keep us from hearing God's voice. When the clouds clear, we find His light shining brightly, offering an answer from heaven. Let us praise Him in the storm today. May our voices not be silent when we feel silence is our answer. He is always there.

Share your experience now at
HungerNoMoreBook.com.

OCTOBER 6

"Help me, LORD my God;
save me according to your unfailing love."
—Psalm 109:26

In our worst moments, all we can sometimes cry is, "Help!" There is no time for a formal address or a longer memo. We need a response and we need it now. The Psalms occasionally even take this direct approach, as we read, "Help me, LORD my God; save me according to your unfailing love." When failure appears imminent, we call our to our God of unfailing love.

The end of the rope stops in the palm of God. When we are ready to fall, we feel His hand around us, offering hope when we need help. His love offers a sure foundation we can build our lives upon. He is our help. Our help is found in His perfect, unmatched love.

Share your experience now at
HungerNoMoreBook.com.

OCTOBER 7

"He stands at the right hand of the needy, to save their lives from those who would condemn them."
—Psalm 109:31

Have you ever wondered why God cares for the needy? Why is there a special place in His heart for the oppressed? Does the author of salvation enjoy providing salvation to those who need it most? Might the Lord Most High most enjoy redeeming those who cry out to Him the loudest? The psalmist informs us that "he stands at the right hand of the needy, to save their lives from those who would condemn them."

Regardless of the precise reasons, it is clear God stands with those left to stand alone. Should we not seek to do the same? When we find a friend in need, should we not work to help meet the need? Let us show the Lord's love to others today.

Share your experience now at
HungerNoMoreBook.com.

"The LORD has sworn and will not change his mind."
—Psalm 110:4

We constantly change our minds. Our tastes regarding food, fashion, and favorites of all types shift like the sands of the seashore. The natural tendency is to think God does the same. Maybe He'll love us for a few years, then change His mind? Perhaps He'll freely offer salvation today, but who knows about tomorrow?

But God is perfect. He has no need to change: "The LORD has sworn and will not change his mind." What He decrees is eternal. He has never needed to change His mind because He has never made a bad decision. We can trust His promises now and forever. He is our perfect Father. His mind nor His heart for us will never change.

Share your experience now at
HungerNoMoreBook.com.

OCTOBER 9

"Great are the works of the LORD;
they are pondered by all who delight in them."
—Psalm 111:2

When someone treats us well, it stands out. We find their service hard to forget. What is true of other people is far more true of God: "Great are the works of the LORD: they are pondered by all who delight in them." When He rescues, we remember. When He provides, we ponder.

This is the attitude of those who love God. We cannot help but find joy in the Lord's faithfulness to direct our steps. We may stumble, but we never fall. We may struggle, yet we never need to lose the battle. The Lord guides and provides for our needs. Our only fitting response is worship. We honor Him with our words as well as our lives. May we remember His great works today.

Share your experience now at
HungerNoMoreBook.com.

OCTOBER 10

"Blessed are those who fear the LORD,
who find great delight in his commands."
—Psalm 112:1

When our parents gave us rules to live by, we didn't always like the boundaries they set. We pushed and broke their principles at times to do as we wished. When we did, we found there were reasons we were not to stand on chairs or walk through the house without wiping the mud from our feet.

What was true of our parents' rules is also true of God. He does not give us commands without reason. We are not to reject them, but rejoice in them. The psalmist reveals, "Blessed are those who fear the LORD, who find great delight in his commands." When we find joy in His ways, we find blessing. If we wish to experience God's goodness, we are to trust in His goodness.

Share your experience now at
HungerNoMoreBook.com.

OCTOBER 11

"From the rising of the sun to the place where it sets,
the name of the LORD is to be praised."
—Psalm 113:3

The sunrise begins our day, the sunset concludes it. From the perspective of the psalmist, during all our waking hours, we are to worship the Lord: "From the rising of the sun to the place where it sets, the name of the LORD is to be praised." This all-consuming view of adoring God convicts us to use every waking moment to His glory.

What habits stand in the way of honoring God with every moment today? Do they include certain places we frequent or games we play? Do we need to change the media we digest or the substances we consume? These difficult questions are worth asking ourselves, as worship must be our top priority. May we strive to worship God every moment today.

Share your experience now at
HungerNoMoreBook.com.

*"Tremble, earth, at the presence of the Lord,
at the presence of the God of Jacob."*
—Psalm 114:7

The Lord created nature and controls it. Every wave is under His authority. The gentle breeze we enjoy moves by the permission of God. In a poetic way, the psalmist commands creation, teaching, "Tremble, earth, at the presence of the Lord, at the presence of the God of Jacob." The Maker of heaven and earth is also its Master.

When we see the beauty of a flower or the majesty of the sunrise, we find the artistry of our heavenly Father at work. Artists paint to reflect the art of the Divine Artist. Sculptors sculpt interpretations of what the Lord has crafted in creation. But nothing compares with God's creative powers. Let us rejoice in His creation of our world and our lives today.

Share your experience now at
HungerNoMoreBook.com.

"Not to us, Lord, not to us
but to your name be the glory."
—Psalm 115:1

The gods of this world consist of created things. Whether a statue or a mountain, the human-made deities of our planet are nothing more than items which people give allegiance. Many times, our idols consist not only of created things, but our own lives. We might think it ridiculous to bow to a statue, yet look to ourselves as the answer to our own problems.

God's perspective is clear. The psalmist wrote, "Not to us, LORD, not to us but to your name be the glory." His glory is our goal, not our own. His honor is our desire, not the honor of others. When others speak well of us today, let us say, "To God be the glory."

Share your experience now at
HungerNoMoreBook.com.

OCTOBER 14

"I love the LORD, for he heard my voice;
he heard my cry for mercy."
—Psalm 116:1

One reason we love God is because He listens. The psalmist wrote, "I love the LORD, for he heard my voice; he heard my cry for mercy." We may have to fight for the attention of people, but never for the attention of God. He is available and desires to hear our hurts and heal our wounds.

We sometimes find this supernatural access so overwhelming we fail to use it. Yet we only miss God's comfort when we do. He not only can hear; He longs to hear from us. We are called to come to Him with our needs. He will listen; He will hear. When he hears, He will provide. Call to Him. He will answer your call for mercy today.

Share your experience now at
HungerNoMoreBook.com.

October 15

"Return to your rest, my soul,
for the LORD has been good to you."
—Psalm 116:7

Have you ever found it difficult to sleep at night? Entire companies are built around the issue of helping people rest who find themselves too stressed to sleep on their own. Perhaps this is why the psalmist wrote, "Return to your rest, my soul, for the LORD has been good to you." There was comfort in the fact that God's nature was good.

Our bodies may struggle with rest, but our souls need not follow. The Lord's goodness provides a pillow upon which we can rest our heads. There is no reason to toss and turn; in Him we find only soothing relief. Let us take our worries to Him today. He has been good to us. In Him, our souls will find rest.

Share your experience now at
HungerNoMoreBook.com.

OCTOBER 16

"For great is his love toward us."
—Psalm 117:2

God does not love us just a little; He loves us a lot. The psalmist noted, "For great is his love toward us." His love is higher than the highest mountain and deeper than the deepest ocean. This knowledge leads us to thanksgiving, that we may praise the Lord.

Our Father's love for us was displayed most clearly through the cross of Christ. There our Lord stretched out His bloodstained hands to say, "I love you this much!" This priceless love cost Jesus His life. The joyous love we experience is the result of His painful experience. Let us not forget nor neglect His great love. Let us embrace it and share it with all we meet. May many others come to know His "love toward us."

Share your experience now at
HungerNoMoreBook.com.

October 17

"The LORD is with me; I will not be afraid.
What can mere mortals do to me?"
—Psalm 118:6

The person who knows God fears no person. Why not? "The LORD is with me; I will not be afraid. What can mere mortals do to me?" Every person we face is powerless in comparison with our God. Our concern is not the size of those who oppose us; we must only concern ourselves with the size of our God.

There is a godly confidence that can exist in the life of the person who knows the Lord. We understand the reality of evil and the conflicts of this world. Yet we do not live in fear of those in this world. We fear the Lord. He holds control over today and all eternity. Let us not fear our problems; let us fear God.

Share your experience now at
HungerNoMoreBook.com.

OCTOBER 18

"The LORD is my strength and my defense;
he has become my salvation."
—Psalm 118:14

A successful military strategy includes an effective offense and defense. God is both. As the psalmist shares, "The LORD is my strength and my defense; he has become my salvation." We can turn to our Father to lead us into battle and to protect us during battle. In either situation, it is His power that saves.

Too often, our temptation is to wage battle in our own strength, turning to God only as a last resort. We surrender to God, but we do not start with Him. Instead, let us begin each day counting on His ability rather than our own abilities. When we do, we'll find help in all of life's battles. The Lord will serve as our salvation.

Share your experience now at
HungerNoMoreBook.com.

OCTOBER 19

"Blessed is he who comes in the name of the LORD."
—Psalm 118:26

Our friends in the faith are friends who inspire us faith. We often find confidence in the community of our believing friends. We may not share the same lineage, but we share the same Lord. When we live together in faith, we find, "Blessed is he who comes in the name of the LORD."

This psalm also found a special significance on another occasion—Christ's triumphal entry into Jerusalem. On the day we call Palm Sunday, Jesus entered the city to these same words. He was seen as the Messiah who had come in the name of the LORD. This Messiah empowers our lives today, by His Spirit and through our spiritual family. Let us live this blessed life today.

Share your experience now at
HungerNoMoreBook.com.

OCTOBER 20

"Blessed are those whose ways are blameless,
who walk according to the law of the LORD."
—Psalm 119:1

A close walk with God is its own blessing. When we follow His ways, we experience an intimacy with the Lord that invigorates our lives. Perhaps this is why the psalmist wrote, "Blessed are those whose ways are blameless, who walk according to the law of the LORD." He knew a holy life with a holy God led to a life blessed by God.

This blessing is not automatic. We must give up much in this world to walk according to the ways of our world's Creator. Others will misunderstand or even mock. Yet what matters to the Lord must matter most. Let us not strive to please ourselves but to please our God. In His ways we find blessing.

Share your experience now at
HungerNoMoreBook.com.

October 21

"How can a young person stay on the path of purity?
By living according to your word."
—Psalm 119:9

Purity is more than physical; it is also spiritual. The answer to purity in our youth is obedience to the Word of God. To obey it, we must know it. To know it, we must study it. It is ultimately study that begins the pathway to purity. Wisdom guides us along purity's path.

Those who are young must be encouraged to learn rather than lust. In learning, we discover God's ways and why they matter. When we understand right from wrong, we can discern pure ways in an evil world. If the choices are clear, we can make a clear choice. The path of purity is made clear by the lamp of Scripture. Let us seek purity by living according to God's Word.

Share your experience now at
HungerNoMoreBook.com.

October 22

*"Open my eyes that I may see
wonderful things in your law."*
—Psalm 119:18

Reading Scripture is not enough; we must also understand it. True understanding comes from the Lord. This is why the psalmist wrote, "Open my eyes that I may see wonderful things in your law." When the Author of Scripture opens our eyes to Scripture, we see it as He intends for us to see.

Further, we are told God's words are "wonderful." They are not a burden, but a blessing. They are joy, not sorrow. They are life, not death. Our Father offers words of life to those who would read them, but readers must have their eyes opened by the Lord. Pray that God would open your eyes to His words today. May you see the wonderful things in His law.

Share your experience now at
HungerNoMoreBook.com.

*"Cause me to understand the way of your precepts,
that I may meditate on your wonderful deeds."*
—Psalm 119:27

We cannot meditate rightly on words we understand wrongly. Therefore the psalmist wrote, "Cause me to understand the way of your precepts, that I may meditate on your wonderful deeds." Proper worship is fueled by proper understanding of God's revelation. We must have both passion and perspective to adequately praise our Lord.

Our human frailty often leads us to pursue either emotion or education, passion or precepts. Yet God desires both. We study what God has revealed, then praise Him for it. We learn God's ways, then give Him praise. Our increased understanding leads to increased adoration. Let us seek to grow in our knowledge of God and our acknowledgment of God. He is worthy of both our reverent study and worship.

Share your experience now at
HungerNoMoreBook.com.

"Direct me in the path of your commands,
for there I find delight."
—Psalm 119:35

Obedience is not easy. Even in the best situations, we find the sound of temptation lurking in the background, calling us to follow desires beyond God's desires. This may be why the psalmist wrote, "Direct me in the path of your commands, for there I find delight." We find joy in the Lord's will, yet need His help to do His will.

This again reveals our complete dependence upon God. We need Him to show us His ways, keep us in His ways, then strengthen us to praise Him for His ways. There is never a point at which we are strong enough on our own. Apart from God, we fail. With God, we find a path of righteousness, a path where we find delight.

Share your experience now at
HungerNoMoreBook.com.

*"Never take your word of truth from my mouth,
for I have put my hope in your laws."*
—Psalm 119:43

Our greatest fear should not be a loss of financial security, but a fear of God's truth. The psalmist understood this and wrote, "Never take your word of truth from my mouth, for I have put my hope in your laws." God's Word is a priceless treasure. We can place our trust in it because it comes from God. As the apostle Paul would later write, they are "God-breathed" (2 Timothy 3:16).

Many of us own several Bibles, yet rarely read words from any of them. Our complacency toward the Word of God parallels our complacency of God Himself. When we find a passion for Scripture, we find a passion for our Savior. Let us put our hope in His truth today.

Share your experience now at
HungerNoMoreBook.com.

"I remember, LORD, your ancient laws,
and I find comfort in them."
—Psalm 119:52

To find comfort in God's Word, we must remember it. To remember it, we must first know it. This order is important, for the psalmist notes, "I remember, LORD, your ancient laws, and I find comfort in them." Scripture offers deep reassurance to those who reflect upon its principles. Yet this comfort only comes to those who know the Word of God.

Do you seek comfort? Look to God's Word. Read it. Savor it. Know it. When you do, you'll find comfort as you look at what you have learned, both as a result of your reading and how your life has changed as a result. Life may let you down, but the Word of Life will not. Find comfort in Scripture's words.

Share your experience now at
HungerNoMoreBook.com.

*"I am a friend to all who fear you,
to all who follow your precepts."*
—Psalm 119:63

There is a special connection we share with others who cherish God's Word as we do. Whether next door or in the next nation, what matters in our friendship are the words of the Lord. We say with the psalmist, "I am a friend to all who fear you, to all who follow your precepts." A friend of Scripture is a friend of ours.

The opposite can also be true. Those who reject God's Word cannot share the same level of friendship with us as other believers. They reject not only the Bible, but its Author as well. Let us be a friend to those who follow the Lord. May we live in joy with all who follow His ways.

Share your experience now at
HungerNoMoreBook.com.

"You are good, and what you do is good;
teach me your decrees."
—Psalm 119:68

When we discover the greatness of God, we unpack a wonderful mystery. God is good, what He does is good, so that His Word is good. We seek what the psalmist requested, "You are good, and what you do is good; teach me your decrees." The higher our view of God, the higher our view of His Word.

Your attitude toward Scripture can reveal your attitude toward the Savior. When your passion for God's Word runs high, your passion for God does as well. Let us not grow weary in our zeal for His teachings. Let us grow in maturity, understanding His ways that we may live according to His ways. May our knowledge of God lead us to a deeper walk with God.

Share your experience now at
HungerNoMoreBook.com.

OCTOBER 29

"Your hands made me and formed me;
give me understanding to learn your commands."
—Psalm 119:73

Since God is our Creator, it is only natural that we would look to Him for wisdom for living: "Your hands made me and formed me; give me understanding to learn your commands." The One who put us together is the same One who places God's words in our hearts that we might live according to His ways.

If we feel inadequate in our knowledge of Scripture, we must look to its Author. He longs to help us grow closer to Him. If we seek to learn, He will serve as our Teacher. He will be our Guide. Let us study under His direction. Let us walk along His paths. He who created us will teach and guide us to know and live His Word.

Share your experience now at
HungerNoMoreBook.com.

October 30

"My soul faints with longing for your salvation,
but I have put my hope in your word."
—Psalm 119:81

Our souls desire to be with God. In fact, the psalmist noted, "My soul faints with longing for your salvation." Yet there is a way in which we can have this longing fulfilled until we find ourselves in eternity with God. The psalmist reveals, "I have put my hope in your word." God's Word serves as the hope of our soul until heaven is revealed.

Does this not make Scripture of greatest value for our lives today? It includes the very words of the God with whom we will spend eternity, and they are available to instruct and inspire us right now. Let us not neglect the Scripture in our walk with God; Scripture is the foundation of our journey with Him.

Share your experience now at
HungerNoMoreBook.com.

October 31

"I will never forget your precepts,
for by them you have preserved my life."
—Psalm 119:93

God's Word can save our lives. The psalmist shared, "I will never forget your precepts, for by them you have preserved my life." Scripture not only prepares us for eternity; it provides guidance for our lives today.

Scripture's unrivaled value must drive us to make it high priority in our lives. We dare not settle for crude entertainment over intimacy with our God. We dare not find satisfaction in the things of this world rather than the Word of the Creator of the world. We dare not seek temporary comfort in place of God's eternal words of comfort. His perfect words guide our lives; may we never forget them, but rather focus on them to direct our steps this day.

Share your experience now at
HungerNoMoreBook.com.

November 1

"How sweet are your words to my taste,
sweeter than honey to my mouth!"
—Psalm 119:103

Honey served as one of the sweetest foods in ancient Jewish culture. Yet compared to Scripture, we are told, "How sweet are your words to my taste, sweeter than honey to my mouth!" The Lord's revealed words offer a taste beyond the satisfaction any food can provide.

Many believers have followed the practice of fasting, going an extended period without food, in order to focus on special times of worship with God. This practice visibly expresses the idea that God and His words are more important to our lives than food. Moses and later Jesus noted we do not live on bread alone, but on the Word of God. Without Him, our lives find no satisfaction. Let God's Word be sweeter to us than honey.

Share your experience now at
HungerNoMoreBook.com.

November 2

"Your word is a lamp for my feet, a light on my path."
—Psalm 119:105

In a world without electricity, torches and oil lamps provided the sources of mobile light on dark nights. God's Word is compared to them both: "Your word is a lamp for my feet, a light to my path." In darkness, light was absolutely necessary for direction. Without it, a person could easily slip or fall from the safety of the intended path.

Likewise, our spiritual path requires God's Word for guidance. Without it, we walk blindly into danger, harming ourselves and those who follow. With it, we walk safely, securely, and with confidence, despite the darkness around us. It can also serve as light to help others. May God's Word be a light for us today and one we share with those walking in darkness.

Share your experience now at
HungerNoMoreBook.com.

November 3

"My flesh trembles in fear of you;
I stand in awe of your laws."
—Psalm 119:120

God's Word can cause us to tremble. Why? As an extension of God Himself, its power is overwhelming. The psalmist expressed, "My flesh trembles in fear of you; I stand in awe of your laws." Here, we find two parallels that inform our understanding of Scripture. First, we find the parallel of fear and awe. To fear does not mean to be scared in this context; it indicates sacred reverence.

The second parallel connects God and His laws. Since His words are an expression of who He is, we discover the same power in them that we find when overwhelmed by the greatness of our God. In reading His Word, we increase our understanding of who God is, leading to a deepened awe for our Lord.

Share your experience now at
HungerNoMoreBook.com.

*"I am your servant; give me discernment
that I may understand your statutes."*
—Psalm 119:125

One of the most important needs in our lives today is discernment. In a world filled with contradictory ideas of good and evil, we require an acute sense of right and wrong to live wisely for our Lord. We declare with the psalmist, "I am your servant; give me discernment that I may understand your statutes."

We must know right from wrong in order to choose the better path and please our Lord. To find that discernment, we turn to the Lord's principles found in His Word. To know His demands, we read His commands. To understand what He requires, we read His desires. Looking for answers? Look to His Word. There we find God and His understanding to guide our ways.

Share your experience now at
HungerNoMoreBook.com.

*"Direct my footsteps according to your word;
let no sin rule over me."*
—Psalm 119:133

Those who control us control where we travel. When we were young, parents led us by the hand to the place they wanted us to walk. God does the same. The psalmist wrote, "Direct my footsteps according to your word; let no sin rule over me." In these words we find that God's gentle direction that keeps us from sin comes from a devoted study and application of His Word.

There is no magic formula to a deep walk with God. We read His Word; it shapes our lives. We live His principles; they change the outcome of our lives. We conquer sin through obedience to His principles, not a formula. Let us walk in obedience today. Let us stay close to God's Word.

Share your experience now at
HungerNoMoreBook.com.

November 6

*"Trouble and distress have come upon me,
but your commands give me delight."*
—Psalm 119:143

Feeling down? Now is not the time to neglect God's words but rather to be nourished by them: "Trouble and distress have come upon me, but your commands give me delight." The response to stress is not less time in God's Word, but more. It is in His commands that we find our joy restored; in them we find delight.

These words not only encourage us when we are down, but can also lift up those around us. A friend in need needs a friend who will point to God's words. We dare not neglect the physical needs of our loved ones; let us not neglect their spiritual needs either. May we turn to God's commands when we are down, that they might encourage us and others.

Share your experience now at
HungerNoMoreBook.com.

*"I rise before dawn and cry for help;
I have put my hope in your word."*
—Psalm 119:147

We tend to wake up early when something is important. A key meeting or a morning flight motivate us to rise from bed before the sun rises. The psalmist had this idea of priority in mind when writing, "I rise before dawn and cry for help; I have put my hope in your word." The problem was untold but the solution was clear—hope in God's Word.

A common attitude toward the Bible is to read it "when we have the time." Yet God is clear that we are to "make time" for His words. Just as we would plan ahead for a major event, we must diligently pursue time in Scripture for it to take place. Let's make time for God's Word today.

Share your experience now at
HungerNoMoreBook.com.

November 8

*"Your compassion, LORD, is great;
preserve my life according to your laws."*
—Psalm 119:156

We tend to view God and His words as two distinct issues. Yet the psalmist spoke of them another way: "Your compassion, LORD, is great; preserve my life according to your laws." God and His laws are structured in a clear parallel that interchanges one with the other. In other words, time in God's Word is time with God.

Many people go to great lengths to discover God's will or to hear His voice. Yet we only need to open His Book. There is no need to chant special words or travel to a sacred destination. His voice is clear. We are called to read it, rejoice in it, and to walk in its ways. Its teachings are compassionate and change lives, just like its Author.

Share your experience now at
HungerNoMoreBook.com.

NOVEMBER 9

*"I obey your precepts and your statutes,
for all my ways are known to you."*
—Psalm 119:168

One reason we are called to follow God's teachings is because He knows everything about us: "I obey your precepts and your statutes, for all my ways are known to you." He sees our weaknesses and sinning failures. Our only hope is to trust in His grace, to devote our lives to His ways.

We are imperfect people serving a perfect God. We don't begin by reaching out to Him; He reaches out to us first. His ways are higher than our ways. Our goal is to conform to His perfect will for our lives, not for Him to conform to ours. Let us live mindful that He is our God. His ways are far better our ways. Let us follow His Word today.

Share your experience now at
HungerNoMoreBook.com.

"May my lips overflow with praise,
for you teach me your decrees."
—Psalm 119:171

In the concluding section of the longest psalm, we find what we would expect—an intense focus on praise to God. In the words of the psalmist, "May my lips overflow with praise, for you teach me your decrees."

Yet there is one unexpected twist in these words. We find praise because of God's teaching. Perhaps this is partly due to the fact that our overflow of praise is a result of our deepened understanding of God's Word. It is when we know Him more intimately that we worship Him more intensely. Let us look to His Word to guide our worship. As we see Him more clearly, let our lives never cease to give Him the praise only He deserves.

Share your experience now at
HungerNoMoreBook.com.

"I call on the LORD in my distress,
and he answers me."
—Psalm 120:1

It would be nice if God took care of our problems before they occurred. Often He does not. Instead, our daily struggles become a test—one in which God waits to see if we will turn to Him or press ahead in our own strength. The psalmist revealed, "I call on the LORD in my distress, and he answers me." He knew the Lord was His source of help rather than His own strength.

How different would lives look if we looked for God's intervention at the beginning of our problems rather than after failing in our own power? The problems will still come, but our response and results would differ. Today, let's turn to God as soon as trouble comes.

Share your experience now at
HungerNoMoreBook.com.

November 12

"Save me, LORD, from lying lips
and from deceitful tongues."
—Psalm 120:2

The Lord is our protection from those who oppose us. No army can stop His power; No force can slow Him down. When we face the trickery of others, we cry out, "Save me, LORD, from lying lips and from deceitful tongues." The God of truth is our greatest defense against Satan's deceptions.

The devil has been called the father of lies. From his first lie to the human Eve in the garden, he has sought to destroy our fellowship with God. He is mighty, but his strength pales in comparison to the Lord Almighty. With God on our side, Satan must flee. Lies give way to truth. Deceit falls victim to righteousness. Whatever lies we face, let us face them with the God of truth.

Share your experience now at
HungerNoMoreBook.com.

"My help comes from the LORD,
the Maker of heaven and earth."
—Psalm 121:2

When a friend helps us in a time of need, we increase our strength. But when the Lord helps us, we receive unlimited power. We can say with the psalmist, "My help comes from the LORD, the Maker of heaven and earth." Nothing on earth can stand against the Creator of the earth. No weapon can prosper against our God.

This world tells us to find the power within ourselves. God's Word teaches otherwise. It is the Lord's power that gives the ability to overcome. His Spirit enables our spirits to stand in the face of adversity. We dare not look to ourselves for the victory, but our Maker. His power is our help in time of need. He is our perfect strength.

Share your experience now at
HungerNoMoreBook.com.

"The LORD will watch over your coming and going both now and forevermore."
—Psalm 121:8

When a mother rocks her newborn baby, she cannot help but watch its little hands and tiny feet. Great love focuses her attention to every detail, every line of each finger and toe. Would you believe God looks at us with a similar love? The psalmist tells us, "The LORD will watch over your coming and going both now and forevermore."

He knows our every detail and cares for our every step. Not a tear falls from our eyes that He does not see. There is not a wound He has missed. Our heavenly Father knows every detail of our lives. How great is His love for us! We need not doubt His compassion; we need only to embrace it.

Share your experience now at
HungerNoMoreBook.com.

"Pray for the peace of Jerusalem."
—Psalm 122:6

God has long called His people to "Pray for the peace of Jerusalem." The city has served as the center of His divine plan for generations. David's throne, the Jewish Temple, and the resurrection of Jesus all took place in this area. Still today, there is a very real sense in which we are called to pray for Jerusalem's peace.

We do not know God's timeline in detail, but we do know He is not yet done with Jerusalem. In the end, the new heavens and new earth will also include a new Jerusalem where He will reign with His children forever. Until then, we pray for Jerusalem's peace; in the future, we know we will experience it. There we will be with our Prince of Peace.

Share your experience now at
HungerNoMoreBook.com.

NOVEMBER 16

"Our eyes look to the LORD our God,
till he shows us his mercy."
—Psalm 123:2

Our eyes reveal the focus of our attention. When we are distracted during a conversation, our eyes look another direction. The psalmist uses the eyes to communicate a spiritual message: "Our eyes look to the LORD our God, till he shows us mercy." The idea is of eyes concentrated on God without wavering. In the mind of the psalmist, there was no other source of such mercy.

This powerful reminder centers our attention on God. Mercy is here. It is found in our Lord. We need not run to another or divert our sight to flashy alternatives. We have His promise of mercy to meet our needs. Let us keep our eyes on Him today.

Share your experience now at
HungerNoMoreBook.com.

*"Our help is in the name of the LORD,
the Maker of heaven and earth."*
—Psalm 124:8

Every commercial promises a new solution to our problems. Whether a car, the latest food, or some other product, the goal is to provide an answer to our desires. While advertisers seek to attract our attention, there is One whose help is sure. "Our help is in the name of the LORD, the Maker of heaven and earth." There is just a single source for the longing of the human heart.

Yet we often crave the latest alternative; there is the temptation of the new, the distraction of the easy, the lure of something better. Do not be deceived. There is no other ultimate source. He is our help. Our Maker is also our Provider. Let us seek Him and supremely Him today.

Share your experience now at
HungerNoMoreBook.com.

*"LORD, do good to those who are good,
to those who are upright in heart."*
—Psalm 125:4

What does it mean to be "upright in heart"? The psalmist simply equates it with those who are good: "LORD, do good to those who are good, to those who are upright in heart." Right actions are an essential aspect of right living. We cannot simply believe the right things and stop there. We are called to live what we believe.

It has been said our lives are the only Bible some people will ever read. If so, what story are our lives communicating? Are our behaviors and attitudes pointing outsiders toward God? Do our words echo the principles of His Word? Let our lives reflect the great love of our God. He will bless those who are upright in heart.

Share your experience now at
HungerNoMoreBook.com.

November 19

"The LORD has done great things for us,
and we are filled with joy."
—Psalm 126:3

When God provides, we praise. Our response reflects that of the psalmist: "The LORD has done great things for us, and we are filled with joy." His acts of mercy result in our adoration of our Maker. Our reflections on His works lead to a response of worship.

What great things has the Lord done in your life recently? Write them down or speak them aloud. As we do, we remember His greatness and glory. We smile at His answers and His timing. Today will bring its own struggles, but the same Father who responded to yesterday's pleas will be there to hear us again in our time of need. Let us rejoice in His answers. Let us look to Him to provide once again.

Share your experience now at
HungerNoMoreBook.com.

*"Those who sow with tears will reap
with songs of joy."*
—Psalm 126:5

Every farmer knows that to reap a harvest, there must first be the sowing of seed. He plants, and then reaps. The same is true spiritually. As the psalmist penned, "Those who sow with tears will reap with songs of joy." The sadness of God's people does not end in tears; it begins there. Joy will one day follow.

In this psalm, joy resulted in a return to strength in Jerusalem. Hard times had resulted in much pain. Yet joy was now the focus, as the Lord had restored it fortunes. We may face a difficult moment now, but this is not the end. God's children will experience eternal joy forever, a promise that brings us joy even today.

Share your experience now at
HungerNoMoreBook.com.

November 21

"Unless the LORD builds the house,
the builders labor in vain."
—Psalm 127:1

Without God, nothing happens. We can hammer and nail, pour a foundation, and construct walls, but life's storms will destroy our efforts in a moment. God is the Master Builder. He not only designs our lives; He builds them. "Unless the LORD builds the house, the builders labor in vain."

How many times have we sought to fix our own problems only to find ourselves right back where we had started? God longs to assemble us from the ground up, shaping us into the work of art He has in mind. Let us lay down our tools and let Him take control. Can we give Him our plans in exchange for His? The result will be a house that reflects the heart of our Designer.

Share your experience now at
HungerNoMoreBook.com.

"Blessed are all who fear the LORD,
who walk in obedience to him."
—Psalm 128:1

There is blessing in obedience. When we are young, we believe rules are made to be broken. We see limitations are barriers to our joy. Yet our reckless choices can lead to much harm. This same attitude can creep into our spiritual lives as well. We see obedience as a problem rather than a positive. Yet it is the Lord's Word that teaches us, "Blessed are all who fear the LORD, who walk in obedience to him."

Obedience is combined in these words with those who fear the Lord. Obeying the Lord is itself an act of worship. We do what God has taught and experience God at work. Our walk becomes steady. Let us not see obedience as punishment, but as an opportunity for praise.

Share your experience now at
HungerNoMoreBook.com.

"The LORD is righteous;
he has cut me free from the cords of the wicked."
—Psalm 129:4

When God rescues us from those who oppose us, it shows His righteousness: "The LORD is righteous; he has cut me free from the cords of the wicked." In the psalmist's time, a farm animal held by cords or ropes would pull a plow or carry supplies. When released, the animal would find relief. This is the freedom found when we are cut free from the cords of the wicked. Such an action reveals God's righteous nature.

The pressure that holds us down during the dark moments of life feels unbearable. Yet such seasons come and go. When these times come, we do not question God. We give Him praise. Facing a difficult time today? Ask God to set you free. He is righteous.

Share your experience now at
HungerNoMoreBook.com.

*"Lord, hear my voice.
Let your ears be attentive to my cry for mercy."*
—Psalm 130:2

We don't ask for mercy; we cry for it. Mercy is not at item on our shopping list, but the longing of a heart in pain: "Lord, hear my voice. Let your ears be attentive to my cry for mercy." The psalmist begged for God to hear and respond. Mercy was not a wish; it was a plea of desperation.

Are you desperate for God? We find ourselves longing for so many things in this life—money, success, fame, achievement, security—but God? He seems to fall lower on the list. May our top desire today not be for what is temporary, but for the eternal Lord. Let us come to Him for our needs and as our top need. Let us cry out for mercy.

Share your experience now at
HungerNoMoreBook.com.

NOVEMBER 25

"I have calmed and quieted myself . . . I am content."
—Psalm 131:2

In an age of abundance, our greatest need is contentment. We have all of what we need and much of what we want. Yet there is always something newer, better, or faster. The answer is not the latest and greatest, but calm and quiet: "I have calmed and quieted myself . . . I am content." The one who finds contentment is truly rich.

Where do we find contentment? And how? We find it in knowing God. In Him, all our needs are met. Love, joy, peace, and much more are all part of our relationship with Him. The how is more difficult. To quiet ourselves requires effort, not in achieving, but in releasing. Not in getting more, but in giving up more. Let our greatest longing be to say, "I am content."

Share your experience now at
HungerNoMoreBook.com.

"May your faithful people sing for joy."
—Psalm 132:8

Have you ever noticed that there are some people who sing more joyfully than others during worship gatherings? Do these people simply like music or is there something more to it? Perhaps these worshippers reflect the psalmist's words: "May your faithful people sing for joy."

Those who love God should not be afraid to say it. Singing allows us an opportunity to express our affection to the Lord in a unique way that other forms of communication do not provide. When we sing to God, He is concerned with our attitude more than our aptitude. Even if we feel inadequate in our musical abilities, we can sing for joy. When we do, we join the faithful around the world who declare His praise.

Share your experience now at
HungerNoMoreBook.com.

November 27

*"How good and pleasant it is when
God's people live together in unity!"*
—Psalm 133:1

There is joy when those who love God love one another. Believers may come from different cultures, countries, or customs, but we serve one God who unites us all. The psalmist wrote, "How good and pleasant it is when God's people live together in unity." The Lord is our peace; He is the One who brings us together.

In a family, we are bound together by a common blood. Yet in Christ, we are bound together by His blood. Our spiritual family can find even greater strength in one another because it is fused together in Christ. His unity is greater and His family will endure forever. Let us rejoice in the family we share in Christ. May we live in unity together today.

Share your experience now at
HungerNoMoreBook.com.

November 28

"May the LORD bless you from Zion,
he who is the Maker of heaven and earth."
—Psalm 134:3

The first verse in the Bible announces God as Creator; the rest of the Bible seems to simply remind of us of this all-powerful act: "May the LORD bless you from Zion, he who is the Maker of heaven and earth." The Lord who appeared to Moses in the burning bush was the One who created the first bush. The God who hung the stars positioned the star the Magi followed to find Jesus.

Our Maker is also the One who blesses us. He does not get us started and then leave. He walks with us each step of the way, offering grace upon grace in our times of need. Let us look to the blessing of our Maker to guide our way.

Share your experience now at
HungerNoMoreBook.com.

*"I know that the LORD is great,
that our Lord is greater than all gods."*
—Psalm 135:5

God is not only the great God; He is the greatest God. "I know that the LORD is great, that our Lord is greater than all gods." Why? Because He can do whatever He pleases. He is Almighty; no one compares with Him. He is Creator; no one created Him.

We acknowledge this belief with our minds, yet often live as if other gods can substitute. For some, it is a particular sport. For others, it is a particular job. Still others find their allegiance to another person or even a religious system in place of God. Yet only God is great. Let us set aside anything that seeks to take the place of our Lord. Let us give Him the worship He deserves.

Share your experience now at
HungerNoMoreBook.com.

*"Your name, LORD, endures forever,
your renown, LORD, through all generations."*
—Psalm 135:13

Some trees can live more than 1,000 years. They have survived the changes of a world, from travel by horses to travel into space. Yet even these aged veterans pale in comparison with the age of our God;He is eternal. "Your name, LORD, endures forever, your renown, LORD, through all generations." Both His name and His greatness will extend into the future without end.

Even better, those of us who know the Lord will be with Him for eternity. This gives comfort to our present moment in a unique way. If we have an everlasting future with God ahead, what problem is too tough to handle? What challenge is too difficult to face? Let us face today in light of eternity.

Share your experience now at
HungerNoMoreBook.com.

December 1

"Give thanks to the LORD, for he is good.
His love endures forever."
—Psalm 136:1

God's love is eternal. It had no beginning and will have no end. It simply *is*. We cannot describe it, though we enjoy it. We cannot contain it, though we experience it. Yet we can give thanks for it. As the psalmist wrote: "Give thanks to the LORD, for he is good. His love endures forever."

Such love is both worthy of thanks and reveals that our God is good. Only the Lord could and does consist of a love so extraordinary that eternity will not allow enough time to understand its depths. We find ourselves overwhelmed that this love can be extended to us, yet it has. Let us embrace His love, giving thanks to our God. His love endures forever.

Share your experience now at
HungerNoMoreBook.com.

December 2

"He remembered us in our low estate."
—Psalm 136:23

Those who stand with us in our lowest of times are those who love us most. This includes God. The psalmist reveals, "He remembered us in our low estate." The Lord not only stood with us; He remembered. He understands our pains and emotions. Because of His great love, He can reach us where we are and lift us up to where we need to be.

This is the joy of knowing God; not that we love Him first, but that He first loved us. Before we knew God, He had to make Himself known to us. We don't earn His love; we receive it. We don't work for His approval; He approves us. Let us remember the One who has remembered us.

Share your experience now at
HungerNoMoreBook.com.

DECEMBER 3

"By the rivers of Babylon we sat and wept."
—Psalm 137:1

There are a few times in life where the only appropriate response is to weep. To weep is more than to shed a few tears. Weeping is the deepest physical mourning we have as humans to express the pain of the human heart. The psalmist shared his deep sorrow in the words, "By the rivers of Babylon we sat down and wept."

He had been taken from his land into a foreign nation as a slave. The familiarity of home life had disappeared. Freedom had fled. There appeared to be no hope for a future. There is nothing wrong with weeping during times of pain. Yet remember God is there, walking with us through every struggle we face. He wipes our tears with His loving hand.

Share your experience now at
HungerNoMoreBook.com.

*"When I called, you answered me;
you greatly emboldened me."*
—Psalm 138:3

There is a confidence that finds its source only in God. When He strengthens us, we can face any battle. With the psalmist, we proclaim, "When I called, you answered me; you greatly emboldened me." His strength becomes our strength and empowers us through the trials of life.

This confidence comes at a cost—we must call out to the Lord. We do not trust in our own confidence or our own power. We do not look inward for our power. We call out to God. We seek His might. When He responds, we walk in full assurance of victory. His power is the power that matters. Our faith grows as it stretches toward our Faithful One. He alone empowers us to serve in His power.

Share your experience now at
HungerNoMoreBook.com.

DECEMBER 5

"Though the LORD is exalted,
he looks kindly on the lowly."
—Psalm 138:6

The Maker of all cares for the lowest of all. Those at the bottom can look to the One at the top for help: "Though the LORD is exalted, he looks kindly on the lowly." His kindness extends to the deepest of human problems, reaching those others consider unreachable. There is no place and no person too far from His love.

Our Lord's kindness toward the lowly is to be our kindness as well. When we encounter an individual in a desperate situation, does our heart fill with love? Do we look kindly upon that person? Let our lives reflect the light of our Lord. May we seek to share with those in need, just as our God has showered His grace upon us.

Share your experience now at
HungerNoMoreBook.com.

December 6

"You have searched me, LORD, and you know me."
—Psalm 139:1

God knows every strand of our being. From head to toe, body and soul, our heavenly Father notes every detail: "You have searched me, LORD, and you know me." He knows us deeply because He designed us. Further, He has designed us for a purpose. We are not simply flesh and bone; we are His artistry, created to fulfill a plan He has prepared uniquely for our lives.

We don't just seek God's will; we *are* God's will. He made us because He desired to create us and desires to live in and through us. Our Lord built us, builds us up, and blesses us beyond what we deserve. Let us seek to grow in the knowledge of the One who knows us.

Share your experience now at
HungerNoMoreBook.com.

DECEMBER 7

"You know when I sit and when I rise;
you perceive my thoughts from afar."
—Psalm 139:2

God knows what we will do before we do it. He understands the options, the conclusions, and every variation in between. We need not explain our situation to God; He knows it better than we do ourselves. As David declared, "You know when I sit and when I rise; you perceive my thoughts from afar."

Rather than explain ourselves to God, let us express ourselves to Him. He longs for our devotion, not our doubts. Our excuses do not please Him; our failures are already understood. He seeks those who realize He is in charge and who will follow His charge. Let us not attempt to hide or excuse our faults and failures. Let us commit ourselves to His faithfulness.

Share your experience now at
HungerNoMoreBook.com.

DECEMBER 8

"Where can I go from your Spirit?
Where can I flee from your presence?"
—Psalm 139:7

God's Spirit is ever-present. This fact can both overwhelm and comfort. As David asked, "Where can I go from your Spirit? Where can I flee from your presence?" No mountain is high enough; no valley is deep enough. God's presence remains with us wherever we may walk.

For those who rebel against the Lord, such a thought convicts. Every sin is noticed; each failing recorded. But for those who follow Him, His presence elicits joy. We cherish His company; we treasure His companionship. We walk with Him, knowing He is with us each step of our day's journey. The difference between whether we value God's view of us or not is our view of Him. Let us cherish His presence today.

Share your experience now at
HungerNoMoreBook.com.

DECEMBER 9

"For you created my inmost being."
—Psalm 139:13

We are not a product of mass production; we are the result of God's creation. As David shared, "For you created my inmost being." His craftsmanship uniquely shapes the way we look, our personality, and our abilities. Our parents, our heritage, and our location are determined by God's sovereign hand, not our own. From our first human cell, we are formed and nurtured by the Lord.

As with Adam and Eve, we are created in God's image. He creates us with unique features, yet we each reflect our heavenly Father. Our lives are of infinite worth to Him; may we give Him the worth He deserves. We are not perfect, but were designed by a perfect Father. Let us worship Him today.

Share your experience now at
HungerNoMoreBook.com.

DECEMBER 10

"You knit me together in my mother's womb."
—Psalm 139:13

How much does God love us? David wrote, "You knit me together in my mother's womb." From the perspective of Scripture, our heavenly Father is involved from the start. He personally and actively participates in our creation. His heart beats for us before our heart even begins to beat.

Could God assign any more value to our lives? He created the world in which we would live, designs us within the womb, and walks with us each moment of our lives. Our only appropriate response is one of worship, loving Him with all our heart, soul, and mind. Let us walk in the love of the Father who has walked with us from the beginning of our creation. He will never leave nor forsake us.

Share your experience now at
HungerNoMoreBook.com.

December 11

*"I praise you because I am fearfully
and wonderfully made."*
—Psalm 139:14

We make much of the One who made us. Our Maker is also our Leader. David expressed, "I praise you because I am fearfully and wonderfully made." Our love for God overflows from His loving creation of our lives. The mystery of human life transcends our understanding; only the Lord could design with such exquisite detail.

If God did nothing but create us, He would be worthy of our praise. Yet He has done far more. The One who designed us died for us. The Son endured the cross to offer us new life, the opportunity to be both born and to be born again. Let us worship the One who gives us life now and for eternity. In Him we find a life that is truly worth living.

Share your experience now at
HungerNoMoreBook.com.

358

December 12

"Your works are wonderful, I know that full well."
—Psalm 139:14

There are two ways to know something. First, we can say we know something we when we understand it with our mind. Second, we know something when we experience it. David encountered both: "Your works are wonderful, I know that full well." His knowing was much more than mental acceptance; it was a knowledge that played a role in all areas of his life.

David had seen God at work from his youth. From leading sheep to leading a nation, David watched God's hand of provision provide at each step. As a result, he called God's works "wonderful." May we have a similar view of God's work in our lives. Let us see what He has done and truly know that He is good.

Share your experience now at
HungerNoMoreBook.com.

*"My frame was not hidden from you
when I was made in the secret place."*
—Psalm 139:15

God knew how tall David would reach, the color of his eyes, and the color of his hair. Every detail was understood by God even before it would be witnessed by David's parents. He wrote, "My frame was not hidden from you when I was made in the secret place." When we begin to understand the intricacy of the Lord's involvement in our own personal lives, we find ourselves in awe.

Who would go to such lengths to create us? Only a loving heavenly Father. The reason He is there in each detail is because He cares about each detail of our lives. Not a moment passes when He is not aware of our presence and our needs. Let our lives honor Him today.

Share your experience now at
HungerNoMoreBook.com.

DECEMBER 14

"All the days ordained for me were written in your book before one of them came to be."
—Psalm 139:16

David understood the implications of God's sovereignty. His words clearly noted, "All the days ordained for me were written in your book before one of them came to be." This word picture was of a scroll that included a journal of David's days written before they had taken place. Ultimately, David did not work to achieve God's will; God used David to achieve His will.

This tension between God's sovereignty and human choice cannot be fully understood from our limited perspective. What the Lord makes clear is that we are to follow Him while He also already knows the outcome of our lives. His wisdom transcends ours understanding, just as His love does. Let us follow His will and embrace His love for our lives today.

Share your experience now at
HungerNoMoreBook.com.

December 15

"How precious to me are your thoughts, God!
How vast is the sum of them!"
—Psalm 139:17

Much of our language for God involves "big." His love, His wisdom, His mercy, His power—all of these attributes and more are "big," perfect in every way. In David's words, "How precious are your thoughts, God! How vast is the sum of them!" David knew in the end that His most expressive words were insufficient to express the greatness of our Lord.

We run into this limitation when we worship God in our lives. We attempt to explain His might and words fail us. We pray to Him with a heart filled with thanksgiving, only to find ourselves without adequate language to praise. Our Lord's thoughts and deeds are beyond compare. Let us worship Him, even when our words are insufficient.

Share your experience now at
HungerNoMoreBook.com.

"Search me, God, and know my heart;
test me and know my anxious thoughts."
—Psalm 139:23

Students often dread exams because they force us to reveal what we know—and what we don't. There is no hiding on the day of a test. We either know the answers or we do not. David asked, "Search me, God, and know my heart; test me and know my anxious thoughts." He did not fear the exam; David was ready for it.

In this case, David did not ask for a test because he knew all of the answers, but because he wanted to improve in his walk with God. The true purpose of an exam is to evaluate and increase our learning. The same is true with God. Let us invite God to examine our hearts today that we may more fully please Him.

Share your experience now at
HungerNoMoreBook.com.

DECEMBER 17

*"See if there is any offensive way in me,
and lead me in the way everlasting."*
—Psalm 139:24

The spiritual life should be one of continual improvement. Ideally, our relationship with God grows each day. Like David, we ask God, "See if there is any offensive way in me, and lead me in the way everlasting." We do not seek to offend our Lord; we seek to obey Him.

When we stop and examine our own hearts, what would God have us to remove? Is there a particular habit that has become a barrier to our relationship with the Lord? Is there a secret sin only God can see? Don't allow it to continue. Let's determine today to remove what removes us from honoring God. May we go on the offense to remove what offends God. Let us follow Him in the way everlasting.

Share your experience now at
HungerNoMoreBook.com.

"I know that the LORD secures justice for the poor and upholds the cause of the needy."
—Psalm 140:12

We would all agree God cares about the justice of the needy, but why? David spoke from personal experience: "I know that the LORD secures justice for the poor and upholds the cause of the needy." He had seen the Lord come to his aid when he was the one in need. He had sensed God's justice for the poor when he was poor.

Both in his own life and in the lives of others, David had witnessed God's care for those in dire situations. He not only spoke of God's compassion; he had experienced it. May we likewise not simply say God cares for those in need; let us serve those in need. May we show great concern to those of great concern to God.

Share your experience now at
HungerNoMoreBook.com.

December 19

"Set a guard over my mouth, LORD;
keep watch over the door of my lips."
—Psalm 141:3

The mouth reveals the heart. David knew this, asking God, "Set a guard over my mouth, LORD; keep watch over the door of my lips." His words required the Lord's security system to stay out of trouble. Our words are a spiritual endeavor; they can give life or destroy life. The difference is the Lord.

When God controls our mouth, it is because He also controls our heart. The two are intimately connected. If we ask God to control our words, He will inevitably begin with the soul. We require a clean heart to speak clean words. God's guard to the mouth covers the heart. The door of the lips leads to the entry of the soul. Let us express words that honor God today.

Share your experience now at
HungerNoMoreBook.com.

DECEMBER 20

*"When my spirit grows faint within me,
it is you who watch over my way."*
—Psalm 142:3

Have you ever felt sleepy while driving? This dangerous mix of weariness and travel has led to many accidents. Likewise, a tired soul mixed with a busy schedule can lead to tragedy. This helps explain why David wrote, "When my spirit grows faint within me, it is you who watch over my way." Our weakest moments are when we need God's strength the most.

As David sat in the darkness of the cave, his eyes would have grown heavy. The cool air would have caused his racing heart to settle down. Weariness began to prevail; his spirit grew weak. It was then he experienced God's grace, just as we do today. Let us not give up when we grow weary; God is there to guide our way.

Share your experience now at
HungerNoMoreBook.com.

DECEMBER 21

"Let the morning bring me word of your unfailing love, for I have put my trust in you."
—Psalm 143:8

There are nights we don't want to sleep. Why? We fear what the next day will bring. David certainly faced some of these times: "Let the morning bring me word of your unfailing love, for I have put my trust in you." Rather than live in fear, David chose to give his trust to God. He did not know what to expect, but knew he could expect God to provide according to His unfailing love.

God's love gives us rest. We trust in the Lord when we cannot see the next day. When we are unable to change a situation, we appeal to the Lord to intervene. He both knows and controls what will take place. His love allows us to trust and to rest.

Share your experience now at
HungerNoMoreBook.com.

"LORD, what are human beings that you care for them, mere mortals that you think of them?"
—Psalm 144:3

Why does God love us so much? As David asked, "LORD, what are human beings that you care for them, mere mortals that you think of them?" We experience His love, yet we cannot comprehend it. It is beyond understanding but not beyond belief. Our Father has revealed His love to us in a myriad of ways. Through His creation of our world to the circumstances of our lives, God had shown Himself as the One who cares.

We may question God's love, but let us not doubt it. He has made clear His affection for us most visibly through the cross, extending His arms wide to reveal; "This is how much I love you." He lives to hold us in His loving arms today.

Share your experience now at
HungerNoMoreBook.com.

DECEMBER 23

"Blessed is the people whose God is the LORD."
—Psalm 144:15

God blesses those who follow Him. He also blesses communities of people who follow Him. What began through Israel and now extends to the church is a unique blessing of God upon those who follow the Lord gathered together: "Blessed is the people whose God is the LORD."

When a group of people who worship the Lord unite, it pleases the heart of God. Our gatherings are a small glimpse of the heavenly reality that will be revealed when all of God's children bow before Him in eternity. Our collective worship shows there is joy both in our personal walk with God and our journey together. Let us treasure the riches of God's blessings upon His people together with those whose God is the Lord.

Share your experience now at
HungerNoMoreBook.com.

DECEMBER 24

"Great is the LORD and most worthy of praise;
his greatness no one can fathom."
—Psalm 145:3

David observes three key aspects of God in two brief lines: "Great is the LORD and most worthy of praise; his greatness no one can fathom." First, David notes God's greatness. Second, the Lord is called worthy of our praise. Third, He is great beyond all understanding. Interestingly, the Hebrew parallel is praiseworthy and unfathomable. We worship God for a greatness that surpasses our comprehension.

If we claim we fully understand God, we are only fooling ourselves. God can be known, but He cannot be completely known. Now we see in part; one day we will see in full. Even in eternity, we will never exhaust our understanding of His greatness. May we worship the One whose greatness is beyond understanding.

Share your experience now at
HungerNoMoreBook.com.

DECEMBER 25

*"The LORD is trustworthy in all he promises
and faithful in all he does."*
—Psalm 145:13

Trust is sacred. When someone breaks a promise or reveals a secret, something intangible yet special is destroyed. These human betrayals help us to understand what David wrote: "The LORD is trustworthy in all he promises and faithful in all he does." Unlike our broken human relationships, we find One who never betrays us or lets us down.

David certainly experienced his share of people who twisted the truth or broke their commitments. Such encounters made God's trustworthy nature even more meaningful to this shepherd turned king. When others were unfaithful, he could turn to the Faithful One. People may let us down, but God picks us up. Let us trust in His faithfulness. He will never let us down.

Share your experience now at
HungerNoMoreBook.com.

*"He is the Maker of heaven and earth, the sea,
and everything in them—he remains faithful forever."*
—Psalm 146:6

If God can create our universe, He can control it. This was the message of the psalmist who wrote, "He is the Maker of heaven and earth, the sea, and everything in them—he remains faithful forever." The One who made us can keep His promises to us. His power and faithfulness are both strong and eternal.

One reason it is important to acknowledge God's revealed account regarding creation is because Scripture often uses it as a basis for His other attributes. If God did not create, then can we count on Him to be faithful? But since the Lord is our Maker, He holds the power to be faithful forever. We can count on the One who counted the stars to keep His promises.

Share your experience now at
HungerNoMoreBook.com.

*"How good it is to sing praises to our God,
how pleasant and fitting to praise him!"*
—Psalm 147:1

Why should we sing praises to the Lord? The psalmist offers a multitude of reasons: "How good it is to sing praises to our God, how pleasant and fitting to praise him!" Here we are told that to sing praise is good, pleasant, and fitting. These three related terms offer strong insight into why we worship our Father.

It is good to sing praise in the sense that it is the right, noble thing to do. To sing praise is also pleasant. Singing can encourage those around us and honor our Lord. Finally, it is fitting. The only appropriate acknowledgment of the Lord who has created and blessed us is to sing His praise. Let's not just speak of God; let's sing to Him.

Share your experience now at
HungerNoMoreBook.com.

*"He determines the number of the stars
and calls them each by name."*
—Psalm 147:4

Each time they use a newly-developed telescope to view the realms of space, scientists estimate a larger number of stars. The number is now so vast that our minds cannot comprehend it. Yet the Lord who created us also "determines the number of the stars and calls them each by name." He set them in place and knows them personally.

This picture of God's creative power highlights what we already know—God is a powerful Creator. Yet it also reveals a loving Creator. He doesn't paint the sky without purpose. His design reveals an intimate care for what He creates, including our lives. He has not only made us—He loves us. Let us worship the One who numbers the stars and knows our hearts.

Share your experience now at
HungerNoMoreBook.com.

DECEMBER 29

"Let them praise the name of the LORD,
for his name alone is exalted."
—Psalm 148:13

God's people are to praise Him and Him alone. Why? "His name alone is exalted." No other compares to Him. The psalmist calls angels, moon, stars, and skies to worship the Lord. Mountains, stones, clouds, rain, and snow are also singled out by name to glorify the name of God. All of creation is challenged to reflect its Maker's glory.

He doesn't stop there. Kings, princes, all rulers, and people of all ages are compelled to praise the Lord. Our all-powerful God creates all of creation. There is no other adequate response but worship. We have nothing else to offer God but the life He has given us. Let us give Him praise and live a life that honors Him today.

Share your experience now at
HungerNoMoreBook.com.

"For the LORD takes delight in his people;
he crowns the humble with victory."
—Psalm 149:4

How does God feel about His children? The psalmist observes, "For the LORD takes delight in his people; he crowns the humble with victory." He not only loves us; He delights in us. We are not a chore to endure; we are children to enjoy.

God also speaks of His people as being humble. Humility stands as a required trait of those who bring delight to the Lord. Let us wind down our year with a look back and a look forward. How did we grow in humility? In what ways could we continue to increase our humility in the days ahead? Let us live as those in whom God delights that He may crown us with victory. Let us walk before Him in humility.

Share your experience now at
HungerNoMoreBook.com.

December 31

"Let everything that has breath praise the LORD."
—Psalm 150:6

It is only fitting that the final psalm would command readers to praise the Lord. What may come as a surprise, however, is the audience of those who are to give Him worship: "Let everything that has breath praise the LORD." In context, many musical instruments are named. The idea is that every noise and every sound should give glory to God.

Many churches debate over which instruments are acceptable for worship. God ends the discussion with "all of the above." His desire is not for any one instrument but for every instrument. He desires the praise of every person. He seeks the honor of every flute, horn, and drum. Let us obey His words this day. Let us live in praise to the Lord.

Share your experience now at
HungerNoMoreBook.com.

378

HUNGER NO MORE

Book + Community = Saved Lives and Changed Lives

Every time you purchase a copy of *Hunger No More*, a person in need receives help to meet their physical needs. The Christian fair trade organization WorldCrafts serves to empower those in developing nations with employment opportunities in over 30 nations so they can feed their families, escape slavery and exploitation, and receive the dignity of meaningful work. Many of their artisans also focus particular areas of need, such as former trafficking victims, those affected by disability, or families affected by HIV/AIDS.

HERE'S HOW IT WORKS . . .

1. You purchase a copy of *Hunger No More*.
2. Read today's entry (starting 1/1/2013).
3. Communicate your response at HungerNoMoreBook.com (on your computer, phone, tablet, or other device).
4. Share your response with your friends

and ask them to purchase a copy of *Hunger No More*.

Soon, we'll be reading reflections of how God is working in our lives with a community of friends all around the world.

At the same time, we'll also be helping contribute to save and empower the lives of others in some of the world's poorest nations.

If we all give a little, we can change a lot.

"Then the righteous will answer him,
'Lord, when did we see you hungry and feed you,
or thirsty and give you something to drink?
When did we see you a stranger and invite you in,
or needing clothes and clothe you?
When did we see you sick or in prison
and go to visit you?'
"The King will reply, 'Truly I tell you,
whatever you did for one of the least
of these brothers and sisters of mine,
you did for me.'"
—Matthew 25:37–40